THE **SKOL** BOOK OF
Curling

THE **SKOL** BOOK OF

Curling

for beginners and experts

Ed Lukowich
with Rick Folk and Paul Gowsell

Canongate
1982

First published in Great Britain 1982 by Canongate Publishing Limited,
17 Jeffrey Street, Edinburgh.

© 1981 Ed Lukowich

ISBN 0 86241 024 X

Typeset by Scottish Studios and Engravers Ltd.
Printed and bound in Scotland by Bell and Bain Limited.

To curlers everywhere

SKOL

Over the past few years, Ind Coope Alloa Brewery Company has been involved to a great extent with curling in the form of the Edinburgh International Curling championship, which has been backed by Skol and the Scotsman since 1974.

Steeped in tradition this event originated as the World's Tournament — one of the first curling competitions ever played in Scotland. Over the years it has attracted many top players; Otto Danielli, Kerry Burtnyk, Jurg Tanner, Al Hackner, Soren Grahm and Peter Attinger on the international side, as well as Scots, Bill Muirhead, Jim Waddell, Colin Hamilton, Ken Horton, Jimmy Bryson and Graeme Adam amongst many others.

More recently, the Skol has been associated with grass roots curling through the Skol Rinks Championship, a national championship for club curlers. Around 1800 Scots each year compete for the coveted silver Targe, which was first presented in 1879.

Skol is pleased to increase its involvement with the sport by sponsoring this book, which goes a long way towards explaining the intricacies of the game to novices and gives tips to more experienced players. It is to be hoped it will also encourage more participation in what must be considered as one of our major national sports.

Contents

Preface

For years I have thought there should be a definitive book on curling applicable to the novice, intermediate, or expert. Now, together with Paul and Rick, I have compiled a book to be just that. In the first section, the beginner will receive a step-by-step introduction to the game. The second section is geared towards those who can now curl but are looking for ways to improve their game. In the third section, we have put together ideas on strategy and various other tactical approaches to the game which can be used by even the most proficient player.

Curling is a game which can be enjoyed by people of all ages and types. A team sport which encourages comradeship, curling offers exciting competition while maintaining a sense of fair play.

There is no absolute in curling. This book will show several techniques which can be employed to develop the same skill. We make recommendations, but it is the reader's choice which method or style is best suited to his or her curling needs.

We hope that you will find this book helpful in the development of your curling career, and we hope it will bring you enjoyment.

Acknowledgments

The authors wish to express their appreciation to the following people for their assistance in obtaining photos: Mike Burns Photo Ltd.; United Press Canada; Canadian Press; Steve Herbert, Calgary; Gordon Nate, Calgary; Frank O'Connor, *Cranbrook News*; Larry Wood, *Calgary Herald*; Al Dahl and Larry Wong, *Calgary Sun*; Al Panzeri, *Medicine Hat News*; Norman Wilson; *Glasgow Herald*; Cowper & Co. and Wilson Groat.

We also wish to thank Warren Hansen, Curl Canada; Ray Turnbull, Champions Curling Programme; Don Finkbeiner, Winnipeg; Mike Chernoff, Calgary; Doug Maxwell, Maxwell Productions, Toronto; and Jeff Rayman, editing and creative consultant.

About the authors

Ed Lukowich — *Calgary, Alberta*
One of Canada's curling superstars, "Fast Eddy" has been curling since the age of six. He is a titleholder in many major events: former Canadian High School champion; winner of the 1978 Canadian Brier; CBC Curling Classic; World Open; and six-time provincial Brier finalist.

Rick Folk — *S̆askatoon, Saskatchewan*
One of the greatest "draw men" in curling, Rick's career is championship style all the way. He has been 1980 Air Canada Silver Broom champion and three-time Saskatchewan Brier representative, as well as Canadian Mixed champion.

Paul Gowsell — *Calgary, Alberta*
The most publicised and exciting curler on the professional circuit, Gowsell's impact has been tremendous. His victories include 1976 and 1978 Alberta Tankard, and winner of ten major cash bonspiels in two seasons, a record.

Introduction

Curling as it was

The first historical records of curling come from Scotland. More than two centuries ago, curling was already sufficiently common and popular in Scotland to be celebrated in a poem by James Graeme. A primitive curling stone, the Stirling Stone, which is kept in the Smith Institute in Stirling, has the date 1511 etched in its side (although experts suspect that the etching may have been done some years later). It is clear that the Scots refined the game by regulating the size of the ice and the shape of the curling stones. They can also be credited with adding the traditional gentlemanly aura associated with curling.

The game's introduction to Canada is better recorded. Scottish immigrants organised Canada's first curling club in 1807 in Montreal, where they played on the frozen St. Lawrence River. From Montreal, the game spread through Quebec and into eastern Ontario. In the mid nineteenth century, curling clubs were formed in the Maritimes, and when settlement moved west later in the century, the game of curling moved with it.

Curling as it is

Canadians have added their own flavour to curling, particularly by building indoor curling clubs and opening the game to women as well as men. The advent of large cash bonspiels and national championships like the Brier with its Purple Heart raised the level of curling skill in the country and increased the popularity of the game. Canadian curlers took the game to its international pinnacle. Other countries followed the lead of the Canadian masters and challenged their mentors for world curling supremacy.

Today ten countries compete in major international tournaments such as the Air Canada Silver Broom, symbolic of men's world curling supremacy. The current competitors are Canada, Scotland, the United States, Sweden, Norway, France, Germany, Italy, Denmark, and Switzerland. In addition, curling is a growing sport in several other countries, including England, Holland, Finland, Austria and Japan.

The appeal of curling

The score is tied and only one shot remains. The next shot buys either a trip to the final or a "bridesmaid's finish."

Each player knows his job. Shakily, the third holds his broom as a target. The lead and second, tense, wait to sweep. The skip must draw to the four-foot. Steadily, the skip swings back, then slides gracefully out of the hack. The stone is on its way.

With possible victory at the far end of the ice, the sweepers polish the path in front of the stone. The skip and third shout, "Sweep," only to be echoed by the roaring spectators. The opposing team watches in helpless apprehension, hoping the throw is light.

As the stone drifts to a stop, a moment's silence — then, pandemonium. The shot is good. The home town team is on its way the final.

Tension, suspense, drama — they are all part of curling, but only one part. Curling requires the strategy of chess, the angle shots of billiards, the finesse of golf, the teamwork of baseball, the memory of bridge, and the adaptability of tennis.

At the same time, curling is a game for all ages and all levels of skill, You may be a once-a-week curler at the local curling club or a would-be Chuck Hay or Bett Law, working your way toward an international championship. No matter how serious you are, curling can provide a lot of satisfaction. And no matter how skillful you are, there's always something more to learn.

Section 1
The Basics

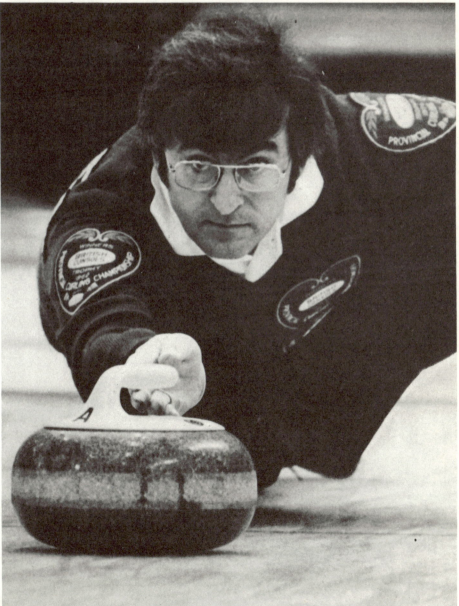

Getting Started

Let's get the stone sliding!
For those of you who have never curled before, the first step is to find a curling club and watch a game in action. That picture is worth a thousand words.

The Equipment

You've seen the game in action; you've seen the playing area and the stones. Now it's time to get ready to play. Locate a sports shop or curling supply centre (usually at an ice rink) and purchase the necessary equipment.

Sweater It should be comfortable — warm yet light in weight.

Shirt Again, it should be comfortable and loose enough to allow unrestricted arm movement.

Slacks The main criterion is four-way stretch for flexibility in the leg area.

Gloves Many types are used. The most important factor is a snug fit so a good sense of touch is retained. Most top-notch curlers prefer leather as it combines excellent feel with durability and prevents blisters.

Socks Sufficient to keep the feet warm.

Shoes The same fit as normal shoes. Any type of low-heeled shoe can be used, but the soles should be adapted to curling standards. If you are right-handed, you need sliders on the heel and toe of the left shoe and a good grip (rubber sole) on the right shoe. Many curling shoes already have a teflon slider; if yours don't, consult a shoemaker about putting one on or use an attachable, slip-on slider.

Brush or broom Only one is necessary.

How to get started

You're fully equipped and ready to start curling. The next step is to join a curling club. There you can get the necessary practice time to learn the game, and later you can become a playing member of a team.

What you practice and how you play are covered in the next section on technique.

4

The Delivery

Curling starts with the throwing of the stone, the delivery. The delivery in curling is comparable to the swing in golf. Stance, stroke, contact, and follow-through all have a major effect on the flight of the golf ball. The ball, like the curling stone, is affected by various external elements once contacted, but the initial impetus is the most important factor determining its path.

The curling delivery can be broken down into several components: stance, swing, slide, and release, as shown at the right.

For the novice curler, the delivery is easier to learn and master if initial practice is done without the stone. The stone weighs about forty pounds and is cumbersome to control until the motions of the delivery are fluid. So put aside the stone for the moment and follow the steps outlined in the next few pages.

5

Lesson One: Short Slide

You're at the curling club and on the ice. The first step in learning the delivery is to begin with the slide. (Left-handers can mirror the instructions which are written for right-handed throwers.)

The Stretch In the ice, you will see two rubber grippers called hacks. As a right-handed player, put your right foot in the left hack. Then, stretch forward with your left leg as shown.

You will feel your left shoe slide along the ice. This stretch is the sliding position: left foot forward and under the body weight while the right leg drags straight and behind. Stretch as far as possible, as this will place your body in a lower position. Do this stretch several times and get the feel of the sliding position.

An Actual Slide Get into a starting crouch as illustrated. Now you're in

the starting blocks and ready to push out. Place your right foot in the hack so your toe is touching the bottom of the hack and the ball of your foot is pressing against the back of the hack. (This will give you the best grip for pushing off.) Push against the hack and slide as far forward on your left leg, as shown, as your balance will allow.

The right foot and leg provide the drive to send you gliding along on the

slider of the left shoe. The stronger the drive, the longer the slide. Try, at this stage, to slide about five to ten feet.

Checkpoint Check your position against the photograph above. The left foot should be forward with the weight of your body over it. The right leg should be dragging straight behind and the right hand reaching ahead for balance.

Repeat the short slide thirty to forty times to improve your balance.

Lesson Two: Balance

Position the sliding foot If, in learning to slide a short distance, you had trouble keeping your balance over the sliding foot, check the position of your sliding foot against Figure 1.

From a front view, your position should resemble the position shown in the photograph below Figure 1.

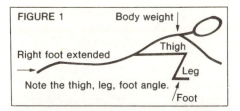

FIGURE 1

Body weight

Right foot extended

Thigh

Leg

Note the thigh, leg, foot angle.

Foot

Hold your knee slightly out from your body. Keep the left foot turned sideways for better balance. Try sliding with the left foot turned at different angles and choose the position which gives you the best balance.

Add the broom or brush In the slide, the brush goes in the left hand. It can be held one of four ways:

● under the arm and across the back
● over the arm
● up in the air
● on the ice.

The most commonly used position is under the arm. Select the method you find most comfortable.

Use the brush mainly as a balance. During the slide, the brush may touch the ice and glide along it, but do not lean too heavily on the brush or it will act as a rudder and turn your slide to the side. It's important to keep your slide as straight as possible.

Test 1 Make twenty short slides, using brush or broom, aiming for a distance of ten feet without falling or losing balance or leaning too heavily on the brush. If you can do it already, that's excellent.

Remember to master each step in the lesson before proceeding to the next one.

Lesson Three: Stance, Swing, Long Slide

Now it's time to start practicing the stance and swing that lead into the slide. Although the illustrations show the curler with a stone, it's best for the beginner to practice initially without a stone.

Stance (*the starting position for the delivery*)

Place the ball of the right foot in the left hack. Squat down, resting on the right heel. The right hand and left foot should be slightly forward. The broom is held to the side in the left hand. Keep the knees pointing straight ahead and the head erect.

From this position, press forward slightly to overcome inertia, then move back into the backswing.

Backswing (*The build-up of power for the slide*)

The right leg straightens to the three-quarter position and carries the entire weight of the body. The right arm and left leg swing back simultan-

eously. The back does not straighten but is simply raised by the leg.

Repeat the stance-to-backswing motion ten times until it becomes a smoothly coordinated movement.

Forward Swing or Downswing (*Getting out of the hack and into the slide*)

The right hand and the left leg come forward simultaneously. Kick the left, sliding foot at the target. The right leg pushes for power, thus transferring the weight to the left foot for the slide.

Throughout the stance and the backswing, all the weight has been on the right foot. With the drive of the right leg on the downswing, the body weight is shifted to the left sliding foot and remains there throughout the slide.

The Slide (*Sliding towards the target*)

Your weight should be on the left, sliding foot. The brush should glide along the ice while the right hand reaches forward off the ice and the right leg rudders straight behind.

Repeat the downswing-to-slide motion ten times.

Test 2 Make ten deliveries, moving from stance to backswing to forward swing to slide in one continuous flowing motion. Do this without losing your balance, and slide as far as you possibly can. You're doing very well if you can slide twenty feet smoothly, maintain your balance, and keep your right hand reaching forward and off the ice.

This complete stance-to-slide exercise should be used for warm-up before a practice or game.

Lesson Four: Choosing the Type of Slide

There are three ways of sliding:

Flat foot: The entire sole slides on the ice. You require a slider on the heel and toe of the sliding shoe. This slide is the best for beginners and for balance; it is the slide most commonly taught and used.

Raised Heel: Only the toe contacts the ice, but the body does not rest on the back of the heel. You need a slider only on the toe of the sliding shoe. This slide is very similar to the flat foot slide.

On the toe (*tuck slide*) Only the toe contacts the ice. The body rests on the back of the heel. Use a slider only on the toe of the sliding shoe. This slide is hard on knee joints and ligaments. Some curlers have used this method for several years and then have had to change to a flat foot slide because of a bad knee. For this reason, this book recommends the flat foot slide.

No matter which slide you use, it's best to warm up properly before you play in order to avoid injury. All three slides are acceptable. Try them and make your decision.

Lesson Five: Add the Stone

You've learned the pattern of the delivery; now add the stone and make the delivery complete. First, however, do several complete warm-up slides (stance, swing, slide). Now do several slides, in the same way, with the stone.

Stance with Stone Grip the handle of the stone with your right hand, the fingers under the handle and the thumb on top. Position the stone in front of your right shoulder. Extend your right arm forward.

While in the stance, push the stone slightly forward to overcome inertia and start the delivery.

upper body lean forward, at the top of the swing, to counterbalance the stone.

Forward Swing Let the stone lead. The right shoulder reaches after it and the left shoulder will stay slightly behind as a counterbalance. The sliding leg comes in behind the stone as you kick (drive) out of the hack.

Backswing Swing the stone back in a pendulum motion. (Do not try to lift the stone; this is a swing.) The height of the swing is a matter of personal preference. Keep your right arm straight during the swing and let your

The Slide The stone leads the slide, and the sliding leg carries the body weight. Remember, there must be no body weight on the stone.

Practice the entire sequence as much as you can. The whole delivery should be smooth, and balance should be nearly perfect. The slide should be straight, not turning to one side or the other. At the very beginning of the slide, the body is quite high. As the slide continues, the body extends more and gets lower. It's called "getting into the slide." Don't skip any one step when you practice; all are important.

Test Three Are you able to swing the stone, slide with it, and maintain your balance throughout? If not, go back and pick up at the point where you lost competence; then work your way forward from there.

If the backswing with the stone is difficult or the stone seems too cumbersome, practice the swing by itself. Don't try to pick the stone up with your back or arm alone, but use the leg in the hack to carry the weight and allow the right arm to do a pendulum swing. The forward speed for your slide is derived from the swing of the stone as well as from the drive of the leg from the hack.

However, it is possible to deliver the stone without swinging it. To do this, pull the stone back along the ice; then use leg drive alone for the thrust.

Lesson Six: The Release

Now it's time to release the stone during the slide. While in the stance, draw an imaginary line from the starting position of the stone to a target at the far end of the ice. Swing the stone straight back and slide toward the target.

Release the stone at a point anywhere from ten to twenty-five feet into the slide; the release point varies with the shot being attempted.

Release the stone from the fingers, simply by opening the hand and letting the stone slip forward. Let the stone glide out your hand; there is no need to push on the release. Contin-

11

ue to slide after the release and let your hand follow through. Keep your eyes on the target; don't look down at the stone.

The turns on the release The name curling originated from the curve or curl the stone makes as it travels down the ice. We say the stone curls when we give it a turn. The turn is controlled by hand action on release. If you threw without a turn, unequal resistance between the bottom of the stone and the ice would cause the stone to curve to the left or the right, missing the target. By throwing every shot with either an in-turn or an out-turn, you can predetermine the direction of the curl.

In-Turn As you hold the stone and look straight ahead at the target, a stone that curls from your left to your right is an in-turn. Start at the eleven o'clock position (photo at top left) and turn your hand clockwise to the twelve o'clock position (photo at top right) as you release the stone.

Out-Turn A stone that curls from right to left is an out-turn. Begin at the one o'clock position (photo at bottom left) and turn your hand counterclockwise, releasing the stone at twelve o'clock (photo at bottom right).

First, practice the turns by sitting in the hack and pushing the stone forward using only your arm. Get the feel of the hand motion for an in-turn and an out-turn.

Then, employing the complete delivery, throw ten in-turns and ten out-turns. The beginning position of the handle of the stone is set in the stance. Keep the handle that way until the midpoint of the slide; then turn the stone gently towards the release position. The stone should spin only one to two complete rotations while travelling the length of the ice.

Practice the release often. It is absolutely critical to top-notch curling form.

Test Four Do several slides to test each of the following points in your delivery. If you can answer "yes" to each question, you're doing well.

Is the stance comfortable and lined up straight toward the target?

Is the backswing relaxed with balance maintained?

Does the stone lead the slide?

Does the slide start high and get lower at the release?

Is the body weight on the leg, not resting on the stone?

Is the back leg dragging straight behind?

Is the slide straight with no turn or drift to either side?

Are your eyes focused on the target throughout the slide and into the follow-through?

Does your hand follow the direction of the stone on the release?

Throughout the rest of the book you will find further hints for improving your delivery. Work at it and try to develop a consistent style. You'll be rewarded with good shots if the fundamentals are mastered.

Sweeping

You've practiced the delivery until it's second nature and now you're eager to play a real game. But wait a moment! That brush you've been balancing so carefully during your delivery is not just ornamental. It's used for sweeping, and, in curling, sweeping is both practical and important.

Sweeping the ice in front of the oncoming stone allows the stone to slide farther and straighter. First, and most obviously, sweeping clears the ice of debris that might catch the

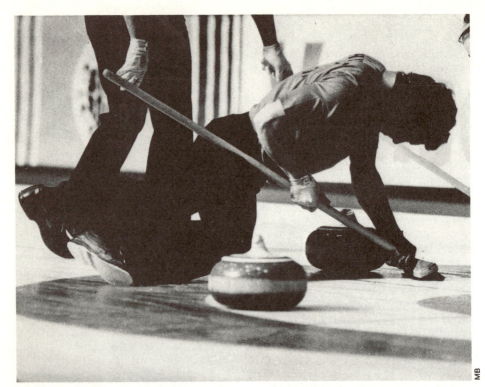

stone and slow it down. Secondly, sweeping polishes the "pebbles" on the ice. Before each match, curling ice surfaces are pebbled or sprayed with water droplets which freeze instantly to create tiny bumps. Figure 2 shows how the stone glides across the pebbles, minimising contact with the ice and reducing friction. Sweeping the ice smoothes the frost off the

pebbles and further reduces the resistance the stone encounters. Good sweeping can allow the stone to travel an extra ten or fifteen feet.

There are two kinds of broom currently used in curling: the push broom or brush and the straw or corn broom (synthetic brooms are also made). Recently, the push broom has gained tremendous popularity, partly because it does not require as much strength or endurance as the straw broom. However, we will examine the use and the advantages of both and then leave the choice to the reader.

FIGURE 2

Lesson One: Using the Brush (Push Broom)

First, assume a three-point stance as shown at top left on page 15. Your weight should be evenly distributed with both legs and the head of the brush bearing an equal amount. Notice that the hands are slightly spread and the handle of the brush rides on the leg-hip joint. If this feels uncomfortable, reverse your hand position and let the brush handle ride on your other hip.

Exercise 1 Position yourself beside a stationary stone. Try sweeping with short quick strokes.

Once you can assume the proper position with ease, practice moving the brush in short fast strokes, keeping your weight toward the head of the brush so the horsehair is spread out evenly as shown in the photograph at the right.

Proper footwork is important in allowing the sweeper to move

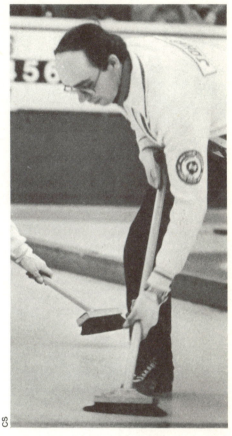

smoothly and evenly alongside the stone. Push with the back foot and glide with the front foot as illustrated at bottom left.

When extra pressure is required for the brushing, get right up on your toes, move your feet farther away from the stone, and lean more weight on the brush.

Exercise 2 Try only the footwork alongside a moving stone.

Exercise 3 Combine the sweeping motion and the footwork. Brush as close as possible to the stone without hitting it.

Exercise 4 Sweep with a partner. Be as close together as possible without bumping.

Lesson Two: Using the Corn (Straw) Broom

There are two acceptable grips for using the corn broom: overhand (above at left) and underhand (above at right). In both cases, the top hand overlaps the top of the broom. The lower hand is mid way down the handle.

Whether you are right- or left-handed will determine which side of the stone you sweep from. If you prefer to sweep with your right hand in the lower position on the broom, then sweep from the right-hand side of the stone. If you prefer your left hand lower, sweep from the left-hand side of the stone.

The broom is held at a forty-five-degree angle with the straw end pointing in the direction the stone is travelling, as shown at right. Your body should be sideways to the stone, head facing in the direction the stone is travelling. Keep your knees slightly bent and your body bent over in a semi-crouch.

The straw of the broom is snapped back and forth in front of the rock. The lower hand acts as a pivot as the top hand whips the broom back and forth. As the lower hand applies force to hit the broom into the ice in the forward stroke, the top hand pulls toward the body creating a snap in the straw of the broom (top photograph, page 17). Then, as the lower hand pulls the broom back on the backstroke, the top hand works away from the body. The two hands always work in opposition to each other.

16

CH

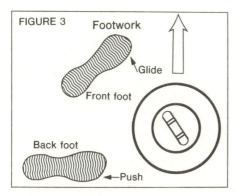

FIGURE 3   Footwork

Glide

Front foot

Back foot

Push

SH

Exercise 1 *Try the sweeping motion while you are standing still.*

The footwork will depend upon which side of the stone you sweep from. Tom (with the headband) in the photograph has a slider on his left foot, so he slides along on the front foot and pushes off every few feet with the back foot. Jim, with the cap, has the slider on his back foot. Therefore, he uses a cross-over step rather than the push-glide.

Exercise 2 *Employ only the footwork alongside a moving stone.*

Tom is using the underhand grip, while Jim uses the overhand grip. The underhand grip allows more power per stroke; the overhand grip allows more speed for faster sweeping.

Tom keeps his front foot angled in the direction of movement. This allows him to watch the stone as it moves while keeping his body turned enough to see where the stone is going. His back foot remains sideways to the movement to enable him to push (Figure 3).

17

Exercise 3 Try the sweeping motion and the footwork with a moving stone.

Exercise 4 Sweep with a partner. Your ultimate goal is to synchronise your sweeping with your partner's.

Curling Tuition

Most ice rinks organise coaching sessions at the request of local clubs and on-the-spot instructors can provide valuable assistance by identifying the diffulties you encounter and speeding up your progress.

Section 2
The Game

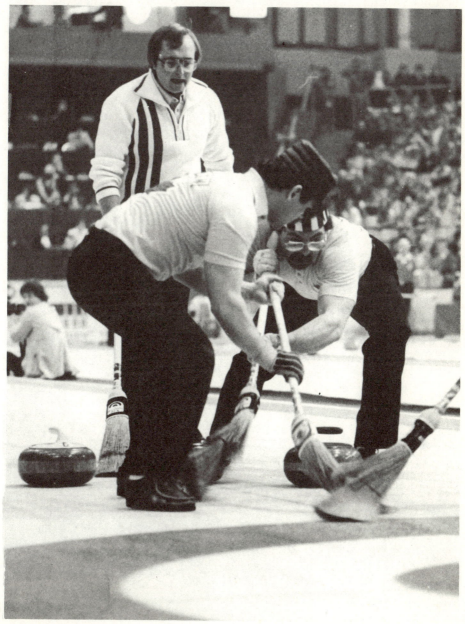

Now that you've learned the basic skills of delivery and sweeping, it's time for an introduction to the game itself.

Essentially, curling pits one team of four against another team of four. A game normally lasts ten "ends," or periods. An end is complete when all stones have been delivered from one end of the curling sheet to the other. In the next end, the stones will be delivered in the opposite direction. Each team has eight shots per end, and the team with the highest cumulative score wins.

The Team

A curling team consists of four players: skip, third, second, and lead. Each member of the team has a specific set of duties.

The *skip* holds the broom as a target for shots by the first three team members, is the main strategist for the team, studies the ice to judge the amount of curl, and throws the team's last two shots in each end.

The *third* throws two shots per end, sweeps, holds the broom as a target for the skip, and helps the skip with strategy.

The *second* throws two shots per end and sweeps.

The *lead* throws the first two shots for the team in each end and sweeps shots.

So, you have a team and every member knows his job. Let's look at the beginning of an imaginary game to see how the team functions in action.

By custom, the game starts with the toss of a coin to determine who has first stone. The winner of the toss has the right of choice. Generally, because throwing last is a strategic advantage, the winner chooses last stone.

Then it's down to business. Both teams play from the same hack, aiming at the same set of rings or house. The skip of Team A indicates with his brush where he wants his lead's first stone to go. Once Team A's first shot has stopped moving, the lead of Team B takes his first shot. After each lead has thrown two stones, the seconds make their two shots, followed by the thirds and the skips. When the skips have thrown their stones and all sixteen stones are at the target end of the ice, the end is complete and the score is tabulated. The stones are then removed from play and the next end begins, moving in the opposite direction on the sheet.

All four members of the team are busy on every shot: one member holds the broom as a target, one throws, and the other two sweep. The team that is waiting its turn to play should also be busy, observing the opposition's shot and learning the curl and weight (speed) of the ice.

The Playing Area

Throughout the curling world, matches are played both indoors and outdoors. Today, however, ninety-nine percent of games are played at indoor curling rinks.

Most curling rinks have four to eight sheets of curling ice. In addition, they are often equipped with lockers, changing rooms, a manager's office, a coffee shop, a lounge bar, and waiting rooms or spectators' areas. However, the heart of the club is that long narrow sheet of ice, marked with rings and lines, where the game of curling is played.

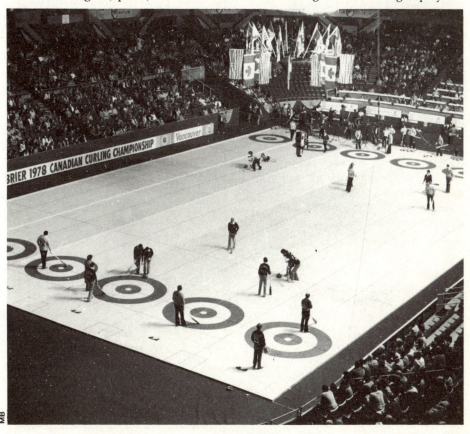

The parts of the playing area:

Sheet The area of play. The sheet is made up of two identical areas at opposite ends of a long rectangle of ice. Each end contains hacks, rings, the hog line, and the tee-line.

Hacks Rubber grips in the ice used during the delivery.

Rings Concentric circles which together form the *house*. Only stones that are in the rings qualify to count for points. The rings are broken down into twelve-, eight-, and four-foot circles, as well as a small button in the centre, so it's easy to determine which stones lie closest to the centre point of the rings.

Hog Line A line drawn across the sheet in front of the rings.

Tee Line A line drawn across the sheet through the centre of the rings.

Back Line The end boundary of the sheet. Any stone completely crossing this line is removed from play.

Centre Line A line running the length of the sheet. The centre line is simply used as a guideline for the players' shots.

Backboards At the very ends of the sheet, the backboards act as bumpers.

Sideboards The borders of the sheet. Any stone striking a sideboard is removed from play.

How the sheet is used

Let's look for a moment at the sheet in Figure 4. The player delivers the stone from the hack (A), aiming at the rings (3). During delivery, the thrower *must* release the stone before it reaches the hog line (1). The stone *must* travel past the hog line (2) at the other end of the sheet or it will be removed from play. The delivering team has full sweeping rights over the stone *until* it crosses the tee line

(4); once the stone crosses the tee line, the opposition can sweep. If the stone crosses the back line (5), it is removed from play.

After all the stones have been played from (A) to (3), the score is tabulated and the stones are removed from play. Then the opposing hacks (B) are used to deliver shots to the rings (6) at the opposite end of the sheet.

The Stones

The game of curling is played with circular curling stones made of granite. Very precise specifications govern the size and shape of the stone. No curling stone shall be greater in weight than 44 pounds (19.95 kilograms) or greater in circumference than 36 inches (91.44 centimetres), which means a diameter of 11.46 inches (29.19 centimetres). The height of a stone shall not be less than 4.5 inches (11.4 centimetres).

The part of the stone that is held during the delivery is called the *handle*. The *striking edge* is a band around the circumference where one stone contacts another.

FIGURE 5

Handle

Striking edge

The bottom of the curling stone does not entirely contact the ice surface. In fact, the stone is ground like a shallow cup on the bottom so only the lip of the cup is actually in contact with the ice. This riding surface, or *cup*, is 5 inches in diameter and ¹/₈ inch wide.

FIGURE 6

Scoring

The object of the game is to place your stones closer to the centre point of the rings than your opponent's. Points are counted at the completion of each end, after all sixteen shots have been played, and totalled at the end of the game. Only one team can count in each end and only those stones which are closer to the centre than *any* of the opposing team's stones may be counted. Each stone is worth one point on the scoreboard.

To get an idea of how scoring theory works in practice, let's look at the first couple of ends in an imaginary game.

In Figure 7, at the completion of the first end, there are only two stones (both black) in or touching the rings. Therefore, in end one black counts two points, one point for each stone. In order to qualify as a possible counter, a stone must be in the rings or "biting" (touching part of the outside ring).

In Figure 8, at the completion of the second end, the whites have three stones in the rings and the blacks have one stone. But rank the stones in the rings in order, starting from the centre: the first is white, the second black, the third white, and the fourth white. The whites count only one point because they have only one stone closer to the centre than the

FIGURE 7
End One

FIGURE 8
End Two

best black stone. The blacks count nothing, but their stone did help them to beat out two possible whites.

So, after two ends the score is blacks 2, whites 1.

Recording the Score

The score in curling is recorded on a board behind the sheet of ice. There are two kinds of scoreboards in common use — the Canadian scoreboard and the international scoreboard.

The Canadian scoreboard consists of three horizontal rows, two of them blank and the middle one displaying the numbers used to count the score. At the completion of each end, markers indicating the ends played, from one to ten, are placed by the scoring team in one of the blank rows next to the number which

represents the team's cumulative score to that point in the game.

For example, look at the scoreboard in Figure 9. The blank row above the numbers is reserved for the black team; the row below the numbers shows the white team's score. Blacks have scored two points in end 1, two points in end 3, and one point in end 9, for a total of five points. Whites have scored one point in end 2, three points in end 5, one point in end 6, one point in end 7, one point in end 8, and one point in end 10 for a total of eight points. End 4 was a blank end (no score for either team) so the marker for it was placed off to one side. To check the final score, look for the last end in which each team made points. Black last scored in the ninth end, and the No.9 marker is above the five, indicating a

FIGURE 9
Canadian (North American) Scoreboard

Black

SCORE 1 2 3 4 5 6 7 8 9 10 11 12

White

Black

SCORE 1 2 3 4 5 6 7 8 9 10 11 12

White

final score of five. White last scored in the tenth end, and the No. 10 marker is below the eight, indicating a final score of eight.

Once the Canadian scoreboard is learned, it is the easiest and fastest to mark and read. However, there is an international scoreboard (Figure 10) also in use. Let's look at the same game marked on it.

Again, there are three lines to keep track of, but in this case the

bottom two lines are blank. The numbers of the ends, one to ten, are displayed on the top line. The second line shows the black team's score and the third line shows the white team's score. As Figure 11 shows, in end 1, blacks scored two and whites scored zero. In end 2, blacks scored zero and the whites scored one. The score in the blacks' column adds up to five, while the score in the whites' column adds up to eight.

FIGURE 10	**International (European) Scoreboard**											
Ends		1	2	3	4	5	6	7	8	9	10		Total
Black													
White													

FIGURE 11												
Ends		1	2	3	4	5	6	7	8	9	10		Total
Black		2	0	2	0	0	0	0	0	1	0		5
White		0	1	0	0	3	1	1	1	0	1		8

Because you have to mark both teams and the totals after every end, this scoreboard takes longer to mark and requires more markers than the Canadian scoreboard. However, it seems to be easier for beginners to grasp.

Rules and Courtesies

Every sport has its rules, of course, but curling is a gentleman's game and curlers are proud of that tradition. The enforcement of the rules and courtesies of the game therefore, is usually left to the honesty and integrity of the players themselves. The courtesies have existed for a long time and are expected. Prime among them is the custom that he who breaks a rule shall be the first to divulge it.

Here are some basic rules and courtesies to keep in mind:

1. When the opposition is throwing, stay off the centre area of the ice and remain by the sideboards. Try to avoid talking that may be heard by the opposition thrower, and avoid excessive movement until the player has delivered.

2. The lead and second should stay between the hog lines when the opposing team is throwing. However, the player who is due to deliver next may stand at the delivery end of the ice, behind the backboard and to the side of the sheet.

3. A team shall not play with fewer than three players. If playing with three, the first two players shall throw three stones each.

4. A strategy decision should take no longer than the three-minute rule permits, and a team should play the game at a steady rate rather than continually delaying.

5. No player shall wear footwear or equipment that will scratch the ice.

6. Each player should be ready to play when his turn comes.

7. Right-handed players deliver from the left hack and left-handed players from the right hack.

8. If the handle of the stone comes off during the delivery, the player may replay the shot.

9. A player who for some reason stops the delivery may rethrow the stone, as long as it has not reached the nearest tee line.

10. A player must release the stone before the hog line.

11. No opposition player shall start sweeping the opponent's stone until it reaches the far tee line.

12. Behind the tee line, the delivering team has the first right to sweep, but the opponents may sweep as well.

13. Only one player per team may sweep behind the tee line at any one time. In international competition, that sweeper must always be the designated skip of the moment.

14. When sweeping with a brush has been completed, clear the brush to the side, rather than just picking it straight up, so as not to leave debris in front of the stone.

15. If you accidentally hit your stone as you sweep it, you should make it known and remove the stone from play unless the opposition wishes the stone to remain in play.

16. When a stationary stone is accidentally moved, it is replaced as close as possible to its original position.

Examples of Rules

A. The draw stone is not entirely over the hog line, so remove it.

B. The black stone has struck a stone that was over the hog line, so black stays in play.

C. The stone has struck the sideboards; it is removed.

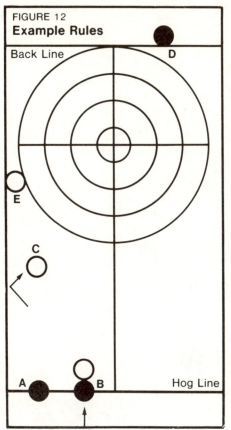

FIGURE 12
Example Rules

Back Line

D

E

C

A   B   Hog Line

FIGURE 13
Clock Positions

6

5   7

4   8

3   9

2

1   11

12   10

D. The stone is not entirely over the back line; it stays in play.

E. The stone is biting the rings but also touching the sideboards; remove it from play.

Often when curling is reported in the newspaper or on radio the numbers of the clock are used to describe the position of the stone in the rings. For example, the stone in Figure 13 is at the nine o'clock position in the eight-foot ring.

Types of Shots

In curling there are two basic bread-and-butter shots: the draw (where you place your shot in the rings) and the takeout (where you use your

shooter to remove opposition stones). There are many more shots, of course, but they're all related to the two basic shots. Figure 14 illustrates the basic curling shots.

Draw a stone that stops in the rings

Come Around or **Draw Around** or **Bury:** A draw that passes close by a guard and curls to hide in behind the guard so the opposition will have a difficult time removing it from the rings.

Double Roll In The shooter raises his own stone into the rings and then rolls into the rings itself.

Draw Raise The shooter strikes a stone in front of the rings and moves or promotes it ahead into

FIGURE 14

A Guard

B Draw

C Come around (draw around, bury)

D Freeze

E Hit and stay (takeout)

F Hit and roll

G Raise

H Double

I Through a port

the rings. This shot is particularly useful if the ice is running very straight.

Free Draw A draw to the rings when the opposition has no stones in the rings.

Freeze A draw up to and stopping against an opposition stone in the rings.

Guard A stone that stops between the hog line and the rings, often to protect a stone in the rings.

Takeout A stone thrown with the intention of taking out another stone.

Double A shooter which takes out two opposition stones.

Hit and Roll Take out an opposition stone in such a way that your shooter rolls over to another position.

Hit and Stay Take out an opposition stone and stay in that position with your shooter.

Peel A takeout shot which removes a guard and rolls out of play itself.

Raise Takeout Use your shooter to strike a stone in front of the rings and promote it to remove an opponent's stone in the rings.

Curling Jargon

When you start to curl, you'll find there's not only a new game but also a whole new language to learn. Like other sports, curling has its own jargon, some of it reasonable and some of it decidedly funny. For example, the rings in the ice are called "the house." A stone is either in the house (on the rings) or not in the house (not on the rings). On the funny side, a stone wobbles down the ice, instead of sliding smoothly, is called a "tea kettle." Sometimes there are several terms that mean almost the same thing. Sometimes

it's not at all obvious exactly what the terms mean. For the beginner who wants to understand this strange new language, here's a glossary of the more common curling terms.

Areas of Play

The areas between the hog line and the back line have specific names as shown in Figure 15.

1. long guard
2. short guard
3. centre guard
4. side guard
5. top of the house (front ring)
6. back of the house (back ring)
7. in front of the tee
8. behind the tee
9. middle of the house
10. side of the house

FIGURE 15

Areas of Play

Delivering the Shot

There are a number of terms referring to the aim and delivery of the shot.

The skip will call upon his player to attempt a specific shot by holding his brush as a target. Of course, the actual destination of the shot will be to one side or the other of the brush, depending upon which way the stone curls.

As shown in Figure 16, if the player released the stone in a direct line with the target A, he *hit the*

skip judges the amount the stone will curl and adjusts the target, his brush so the shot ends up in exactly the right place. In practice, things don't always work out as they are supposed to! Sometimes a stone will curl less than expected, usually because the ice was unexpectedly sloped, causing the stone to travel too straight. In this case, the stone is said to *fall*, or *drift out*, or *stay out*, or *hang*. On other occasions the stone will curl more sharply than expected. The skip may have underjudged the

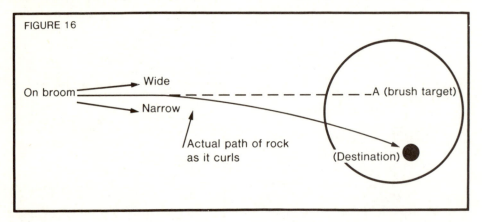

FIGURE 16

On broom — Wide

Narrow

Actual path of rock as it curls

A (brush target)

(Destination)

brush. If his line of delivery was off target, he *missed the brush*. An off-target shot released slightly towards the destination rather than straight at the brush is *narrow*. A shot released even farther off the destination than the brush indicates is *wide*.

The speed with which the stone travels is called the *weight*. A stone released with too much speed and therefore likely to travel too far is *heavy*. A stone released with too little speed is *light* or *under thrown*.

Stones are always released with either an *in-turn* or *out-turn*, depending upon which direction they are supposed to curl. In theory, the

amount of curl in the ice, the weight may have been too soft, or the stone may have caught some debris. In this case, the stone is said to *overcurl*, or *cut too much*, or *take off*, or *grab*.

Other Common Terms

Big End a count of three or more points

Biter a stone only partially touching the outside ring

Blank no score

Bonspiel tournament

Burned Stone a stone accidentally contacted in the act of sweeping. The rules regarding burned stones vary with the situation.

Button the centre of the house

Clean It keep the ice clean in front of the stone

Combination a multiple raise shot

Deuce two points

Dumped see Turned

End curling's version of a period or innings.

Extra End If the score is tied after ten ends, and extra end is played to determine the winner.

Flash a missed takeout.

Flip throw a shot wide of the brush because of excessive hand action.

Front End the first two players (lead and second) on a team

Give the Ice The skip asks for a shot and then holds the broom as a target, thereby indicating the amount the stone should curl.

Going Home playing the last end of the game

Hammer the last shot of the end. If you win the toss at the beginning of the game, you should choose last shot. The noncounting team on an end always gets last stone on the next end. If the end was blanked, last stone remains with the team that had it in the blank end.

Heavy Ice ice on which the stones do not slide easily

House the rings

Hurry sweep harder

Keen Ice ice on which the stones slide very easily

Lie/Lying count/counting. You may be lying counters during the end, but they are not counted as points until the end is complete.

Mate see Vice-Skip

Measure If, at the conclusion of the end, the stones are too close to tell which are counters, a measure is required.

Pebble water sprinkled on the ice surface before the game to make the stones slide better

Pocket stones bunched together offering a nice backing for a freeze

Port two stones separated just enough that a third stone can pass between them

Read the Ice All ice is individual. The skip watches shots travel down the ice in order to learn the amount of curl required for other shots.

Rub touch a guard stone with your shooter in passing

Run a straight spot in the ice where the stone, when thrown with a particlar turn, will not curl and may even drift farther away

Runner a fast takeout

Second Shot the stone second closest to the centre of the rings

Shot Stone the stone that is closest to the centre of the rings

Silent Takeout see Flash

Split the House a situation where you have a stone on one side in the rings and you draw another stone to the other side of the rings

Steal count points when you did not have last stone

Straight Handle a stone delivered with no definite turn

Swingy Ice an ice condition in which all the stones curl sharply

Tea Kettle see Wobbler

Tee a line across the centre of the rings, significant in the sweeping rules

Tight a stone thrown extemely close to a guard and in danger of rubbing or wicking the guard as it passes

Tough Ice see Heavy Ice

Turned narrow of the brush because of a poor, lazy release.

Vice-Skip alternate title for third

Wick see Rub

Wobbler a thrown stone that is not riding on the entire cup and therefore is bouncing from side to side.

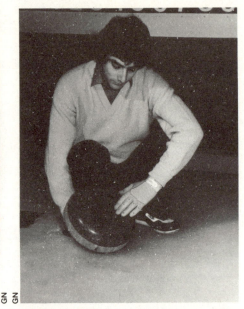

Starting Pointers

Talking curling is fine, but playing the game is what it's all about. Here are a few tips to get you off on the right foot, or slider.

Shooting

1. Clean your slider of debris before preparing to slide.

2. Clean the bottom, running surface of the stone with the brush and your hand and sweep any debris to the side before you turn the stone back down.

3. Learn the skip's signals for takeout, draw, turn required, and weight required. On draws, the skip taps the ice where the stone is to stop. On takeouts, he taps the stone to be hit and may indicate a new spot to roll to. Arm signals can be used to indicate the weight and the turn.

4. Learn the various weights the skip may ask for:

Guard in front of the rings

Draw weight enough to stop in the rings

Hack weight enough weight to take out a stone and send it as far as the hack

Bumper weight enough weight to take out a stone and send it ten feet past the hack. Used as a takeout when you don't want to roll too far.

Takeout twenty feet harder than a bumper. It should hit the stone hard when it takes it out. This weight is used for doubles and for clearing guards.

The amount of ice (the amount the stone will curl) is related to the weight thrown. Guards and draws will curl the most, while takeouts will curl the least.

5. Look at the skip's brush all the way through the slide. Do not look down at the stone in your hand while you are sliding or before you have released it.

6. Complete your slide. Follow through by continuing to slide even after you release the stone. Don't jump up immediately.

7. Slide at different speeds for different shots. On takeout shots slide out faster and release once you're on a good line. On draws slide out more slowly and release with a feel for the weight.

Sweeping

1. Sweeping should start at the back of the tee line and close to the boards in order to give the thrower room to slide. Begin moving with the thrower's downswing and stay slightly ahead of the stone. Move in closer to sweep as the stone is released. It will be easier to judge the weight if you move with the thrower.

2. Don't keep your head down all the time when you are sweeping or you may lose track of how far you have to go. Glance alternately at the stone, to guage its speed, and up, to check the path. While sweeping, always keep the body turned slightly forward so you can easily glance up to judge the distance or catch the skip's signal.

3. When you stop sweeping with a brush, clear to the side, not straight

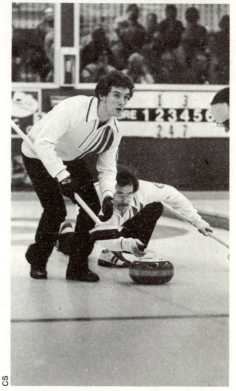

in front of the stone, as debris would fall in the path of the stone.

Care of Equipment

1. Corn broom Store the broom in a cool, moist place when it is not in use. Heat will dry out the straw, causing it to break easily.

2. Push broom or brush Approximately every two weeks, your brush should be washed. Using warm water and soap, wash the bristles and comb out loose hairs and debris with a fork. This prevents the stiffening of the bristles and allows them to spread out during the sweep. As well, there is less tendency for hairs to break off. Too many curlers don't clean their brushes, and as a result too many fine shots have been ruined by a stone picking up a hair.

3. Slider Wear a covering for your slider when walking anywhere other than on the ice surface. Sliders are easily marked by dirt or sand.

Strategy

Curling is more than just sliding stones down a sheet of ice. Like chess, curling is a game of strategy, of move and countermove, of outguessing and outplaying your opponent. Every shot in a curling game is part of the strategy.

Each skip will take a slightly different approach, and it is hard to say which approach is best. However, there are basic rules of thumb for planning strategy, and there are some standard responses to common situations which are worth noting here. But remember, skill counts; the best strategy in the world will not win unless your team can make the shots. The main thing to learn is how to play the percentages, and that comes only with experience.

In choosing your strategy, there are a number of factors which should be considered:

- The score. Are you ahead or behind?
- Is it early or late in the game?
- What are the ice conditions?
- How well are you playing?
- How well is the opposition playing?
- Who had the advantage of last on the end?

Once you have answered these questions, there are still other factors to take into account when calling the shot. It is vital to know your own team; the final decision on any shot may depend upon the personal preference, skill, and confidence of the player.

Strategy is a coin with two sides. On one side are your game plan and your strengths. On the other side are the weaknesses of the other team. Play the strategy that your team is best at, but also play a strategy that will give your opposition trouble. Learn to think a few shots or even a few ends ahead. The old curling catch phrase, "It's not just what you make, but also what you leave," holds true. Try to plan, ahead of time, the kind of shot you would like to leave for your opponent and also the type of shot you would prefer.

The Game Plan

There are two possible plans:

1. Go for the points — Go on the offensive immediately, employing a strong draw game. Try to establish a large lead by the completion of the first half. Then play defensively to maintain the lead.

2. Stay close — Play defensively, employing takeouts, trying to keep within scoring distance of your opponent. Avoid excessive gambling, get

CS

the feel of the ice, and wait for the opposition to make mistakes.

Whatever plan is used in the first half of the game, the second half should be skipped with the aim of gaining control. Try to be even or one point ahead with the advantage of last stone going into the final end. This approach will win you the majority of games.

In the following pages, we will look at examples of strategy in specific situations. You will use the black stones in the diagrams, while the opposing team will have the whites. At the top of some figures, you will notice a black or white stone; that symbol indicates which team has the advantage of last stone.

Using the Middle

The middle is the area in front of the house that leads to the four-foot ring and the button. When you have the advantage of last shot, try to keep the middle open so you have easy access for shot. You should try to build a good end to the sides of the house while holding the middle clear. Then you have an open path to save the end on your last shot if trouble does develop.

The rule to remember: An open shot is desirable.

When the opposition has the last shot, try to close up the middle by putting your shots in front of the house near the centre line. Then, if

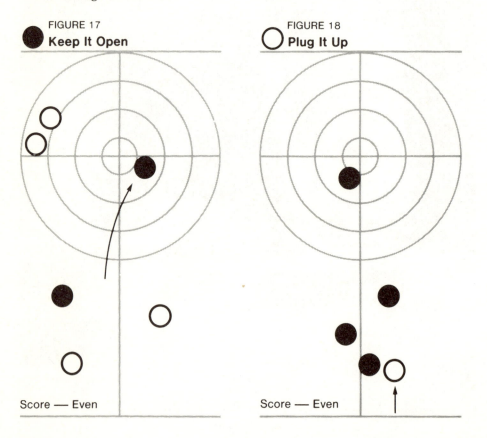

FIGURE 17
Keep It Open

Score — Even

FIGURE 18
Plug It Up

Score — Even

you can get a stone close to the button, the opposition may have a difficult last shot and miss, leaving your side with a steal.

The rule to remember: Leave the opponent a last shot through traffic.

How many points do you go for?

If you have last stone, try to count more than one point on the end. Play offensively, but try to leave the middle open for your last shot.

If, on the last shot, there are no stones in the house or the opposition has the only stone, try to blank the end rather than going for a single point. This way you retain last shot for the next end, and you have another chance to count more than one.

There are, however, exceptions to the rule. If you are comfortably ahead, you may play nothing but hits in order to eliminate any chance of the opposition's catching up. Or, if it is the last end and the score is tied, you need only one point to win, so there is no need to gamble for more than one.

If the opposition has the hammer, try either to steal or to force them to take only one point, thereby using up the advantage of their last stone.

Again, there are exceptions. When you are tied or behind on the last end and you don't have last rock, forcing the opposition to take one point will lose you the game. In this situation, you must try to score at all costs.

FIGURE 19
Play for Two

Score — Even

FIGURE 20
Steal or Force

Opponent must outdraw your shot or allow a steal.

Score — Close

FIGURE 21 **Simple Strategy Summary**

When you have last stone and are drawing into the open house, play your stone (A) deep behind the tee line. This position offers you several advantages. If the opposition takes your stone out, you can freeze up to their stone and still be shot stone. Secondly, it takes the game to the back of the rings, which gives you backing for your last shot and makes it easier. Thirdly, drawing to the back of the house makes it easier to blank the end; stones in the back of the house (B) are easier to roll out on.

When the opposition has last stone, keep your draw shots (A) in front of the tee line. This position gives the opposition nothing to draw up against and means that on their last shot they will probably have to move one of your stones back, a more difficult shot than simply drawing down to one of your stones. Any of your draws that stop in front of the tee line are worth guarding (B) or raising (C).

FIGURE 22
Positioning Shots

FIGURE 23
Positioning Shots

If you have a counter (A) on one side of the rings, draw to the other side of the rings (B). Keep your stones apart; don't bunch them together and give your opponent a bigger target. Make it difficult for the opposition to make a double.

FIGURE 24

Splitting the House

Guards — How to Use Them and How to Avoid Them

When you have last stone and the opposition is playing centre guards to block the middle, it is wise to take their centre guards off and roll to the side for a side guard which is more advantageous to you (A). However, do not take any guards out if you are several points behind in the score. Instead, draw behind the guard and use it for protection in an attempt to score points (B).

When you have last stone and wish to try for more than one point, play a side guard and try to get a side draw game going. Drawing behind side guards is to your advantage if you have last stone, as it leaves the middle open for your last shot.

Don't play any guards in front of the rings if you are comfortably ahead.

FIGURE 26
Side Guard Draw Game

Side (corner) guard

FIGURE 25
Roll to the Side

Score — Close

When drawing around a guard, keep your stone in front of the tee line so the opposition, even if they draw up to you, will not have shot stone (A). If the draw around the guard is too deep (B), the opposition can draw up to you for shot stone — and you have a problem.

FIGURE 27
Drawing Around a Guard

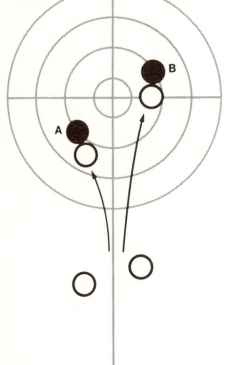

If there are guards in front of the rings and an opposition stone offering a good chance to hit and roll, play the hit and roll. You will remove the opposition stone and at the same time get your shooter behind the cover of guards.

FIGURE 28
Hit and Roll

Early in the end, the opposition has a solid shot stone behind a guard. If you draw to it, there are three possible places your shot might stop:

1. Right on top of their stone for shot stone. Congratulations — a perfect shot!

2. Back of the house. This is too far, an amateur shot. Now the opposition can draw another one behind the same guard.

3. In front of their stone but not yet shot stone. This is the second best shot and is called "missing on the pro side." It is a slight miss that may benefit you before the end is complete. You can tap your stone up later in the end, or the opposition may try

FIGURE 29

Pro Side

to take your stone out and hit it up onto their own stone, completing your original shot for you.

Half of something is better than all of nothing. The other team has a stone (A) behind a guard. You plan to try to come around the guard and take it out. This is an excellent shot if you make it; at worst, you could miss everything (B). To minimise your losses, play close to the guard so you either make the shot or rub the guard. If you move the guard, at least you have missed on the pro side and you have opened the stone up for your next shot. If you rub the guard, try to roll your shooter into the rings (C).

FIGURE 30
Pro Side

Clean House or Dirty?

If you are comfortably ahead in the score, play takeouts to remove all the opposition stones. Take off the guard and roll out of play. Try to give the opposition nothing to draw behind or to draw up to. This is called "keeping it clean" by using a hitting strategy.

If your team is called upon to draw, do not stop short of the rings and give the opponents a guard to draw behind. Mistakes like that lose games.

FIGURE 31
Defense

Score —
Black ahead several

If you are behind in the score, try to manufacture points by making the opposition's shots more difficult. Do this by drawing behind the guard (A) and freezing up to the opposing team's stones (B). This is called "junking it up" or "the garbage game" and is accomplished by using draw shots to keep your stones in play.

Don't be heavy on draw shots if you are behind in the score, and don't play heavy takeouts. Play soft to keep your stones in play.

Attempt to catch up slowly ("pick away") don't take unnecessary risks trying to make a big score to catch up.

Ports

If you are drawing through a port, watch for a possible thin rub on one of the stone in front. A thin rub might be a perfect deflection, sending your shooter right behind a guard.

FIGURE 33
Through a Port

FIGURE 32
Offense

Score —
Black behind several

If you have a stone partially guarded and you want to guard it again, it is okay to leave a port. However, the port should be no bigger than twelve inches, the width of a curling stone.

FIGURE 34
Guarding

To draw between two guards in staggered formation, play the natural turn that will allow your shot to curve through the port. In the diagram, the in-turn can easily draw through the port, whereas it would be impossible or at least very difficult to draw through on the out-turn.

FIGURE 35
Drawing a Port

Double Roll In

When trying to execute a double roll in, play your stone across the face of the stone you are aiming at so your shooter is sliding off the other stone. This gives the best angle for a double roll in.

FIGURE 36
Double Roll In

Taking a Point

It is often good strategy to take one point with the hammer on the first end rather than blanking. It's nice to score early and be on the board. Also, near the end of the game, try to score the even ends as this will set you up for last stone on the tenth end.

Raises

If there are a number of stones in front of the rings, raise your stones into the house behind the cover of the guards. Attempt this shot if your stone is close enough to the house to offer a good raise or if you are faced with a difficult draw around guards.

FIGURE 37
Draw Raise

When you raise a stone, which turn will it take? If you strike the rock dead on (A), it will take the opposite turn from the shooter. If the shooter strikes off centre (B), the stationary rock will be spun according to which side was struck.

FIGURE 38
Turns in Raising

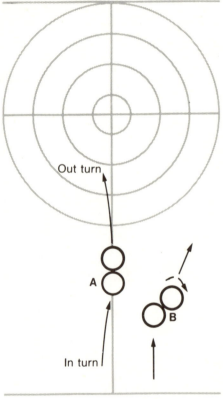

Doubles

There are two ways of making a double in curling:

A. Your shooter hits one of the opposition's stones, rolls over, and removes their other stones as well.

B. Your shooter strikes the first opposition stone; which travels on to strike another opposition stone off centre. The two opposition stones then "split" and roll out of the house in opposite directions.

In trying to execute doubles, it is important not to risk missing everything but to be sure of hitting the stone at which you are shooting.

What You Make and What You Leave

If you have last stone and the opposing team is lying a lot of counters, do not play heavy takeout weight on your last shot. The risk of rolling out is too great, and you would leave the opposition lying too many. Therefore, on your last shot (A), play very quiet weight to move their shot stone back just a little.

When you are in this kind of trouble, the skip should play his personal preference on the last shot. Play your strength, your best percentage shots.

FIGURE 39
Doubles

A   B

FIGURE 40
Play Safe Weight

A

49

When you are lying some counters (A and B) and the opposition has last stone, try to place your last stone to make the opposition's shot tougher. In the diagram, you are already lying two and the shot stone (B) is biting half of the four-foot circle. Draw your shot (C) to the top of the four-foot-circle. Now if the opposition hits your stone at the top of the four-foot, they will not have shot stone (D). their alternative is to draw and that too is very difficult. So you see, it's not only "what you make," but also "what you leave" for the other team.

FIGURE 41
Leave it Tough

Section 3
The Expert Game

First and foremost, curling should be fun. After all, it is a game, and games are played for enjoyment. But as your skill increases, you'll discover a new kind of fun — winning. And you'll find yourself playing to win. You'll want to become an expert.

The expert curler develops his skills to the limit; he wants to be the best there is. That requires work, practice, and critical self-appraisal. It also requires teamwork. The golfer can make it alone, but the expert curler can't win unles he's part of an expert team.

In the following pages, there are a number of tips and exercises designed to improve your individual game. However, the emphasis is on the development of an effective team and of the systems that will make it a cohesive, successful, *winning* team.

Choosing a Team

A winning team consists of four strong players. The selection of players is the most important decision you will make; it will determine not only your success in competition but also the amount of enjoyment you get from the game. All four players should be happy with their positions and have confidence in one another. It's almost impossible to have four players on a team with identical personalities, outlooks, reactions, and time availability. A good team will recognise the differences among its players and use them to the team's advantage. Above all, when you get into serious competition, it's important to recognise that different people react differently under pressure and to accept these differences.

When picking a team, here are some qualities to look for:

In general, look for good athletes who are strong competitors, con-fident, willing to practice, enthusiastic, and easy to get along with. Select players who want to be the best there is at their positions. Not everyone can or should be skip; it requires a special talent and a very strong nerve.

The *lead* starts each end for your team and is extremely important in setting the strategy. Therefore, a lead should have excellent draw weight for placing those first shots. He should also be an average hitter, a strong sweeper, and a good judge of draw weight while sweeping.

The *second* should be a strong takeout shooter, a good sweeper, and a good judge of weight while sweeping. He should also be effective on offensive shots so you can gain the advantage on offence early in the end if need be.

The *third* is the trouble-shooter. he must be able to play all the shots and either turn, and be skilled enough to turn situations in your favour with one good shot. Since he acts as vice-skip, he should also have some knowledge of strategy and good judgement in calling shots.

The *skip* should be a trouble-shooter and a good finisher in all sorts of situations. He must be strong on both turns, on takeout, and especially on draws and have the ability to perform under pressure. He must also be a good strategist and an excellent reader of the ice.

When choosing players, re-member you're putting together a team, not just four strong players but four strong players who complement one another. You're lucky if you have one player on the front end who is very enthusiastic and who can get his teammates "up" for the game. You're very lucky if the other front-end player is calm and reassuring. Add a third who consistenly makes his shots and a daring skip who can come through with the shots that are needed — and you have a winning combination.

Mental Attitude

In any activity, mental attitude is extremely important. To put it simply, if you can conceive and believe, you will achieve. This principle holds particularly true in curling, which is as intellectual as it is physical.

Confidence

If there is one trait common to all winners, it is their confidence. If you are confident, then you have power. On the other hand, it is almost impossible to accomplish a task if you think you can't. Confidence puts you over the bar or helps you score the goal. Luck is involved, of course, but the most confident person usually also has the luck.

Picture yourself succeeding. Never second guess yourself. Believe in yourself, for curling is as much a test of character as a test of ability. Be optimistic, especially when the going gets tough. A team's success can be directly related to its performance under pressure. Even if a team member misses a shot, encourage him; don't discourage him. Knowing that his team is solidly with him, through thick or thin, will help. In fact, it is the duty of every player to reinforce his teammates' confidence and his own. Even vocabularly counts. Eliminate negative thoughts and definitely eliminate negative comments.

Determination

Never cheat yourself by lack of effort. A determined competitor gives 100 percent always. Compete with your-self; in every game, try to top your own best performance. Give every shot all you've got, and never give up. Determination is a hard thing to defeat. Remember, to be the best, you have to beat the best.

Concentration

It is hard to say much about concen-tration, and, at the same time, it is impossible to over-emphasise its im-portance in curling. You must be-come completely absorbed in the game, forgetting all external factors. Don't worry about the other games going on around you, and forget about the spectators. Your own game is all that matters. If you become the shot, you will make the shot. It's a kind of self-hypnosis; only when you're totally absorbed in your game are you at your best.

We've barely touched on the sub-ject of mental attitude, but it's impor-tant enough to fill another book.

Never slight the amount of psycho-logical effort involved in a curling match. Through the constant analysis of your game, both on the ice and in retrospect, you can become a top-notch team. If you then add con-fidence, determination, and con-centration, you can become win-ners.

Training

The legs are the kingpins of curling. Their strength and conditioning make all the difference in the slide and the sweeping, where the body is always in a semi-crouch. A sweeper, playing in three games a day, will travel miles on those kingpins.

Here is a list of sports and exer-cises that help to condition curling muscles:

Swimming The best exercise for body tone. Use legs-only strokes to develop the thigh muscles and gain flexibility.

Jogging use for general conditioning as well as for thigh and calf muscles.

Hockey Great for the legs.

Basketball Good for leg development. Also, shooting baskets gives a good feel for draw weight.

Squash, Racquetball Great conditioning. They also teach a tougher mental attitude.

Golf Good for the legs. Golf is closely related to curling, particularly in judging the weight of putts and reading the green.

Exercises Sit-ups — Strong stomach muscles give the body control and balance.

Flexibility stretches — You need flexibility for a smooth delivery. A fifteen-minute stretching programme each day is beneficial.

Weights Working out with weights adds strength but does not increase shooting ability in curling. Curling, like golf, does not require a strong weights programme. The skip, who has to play with finesse, doesn't need bulk muscle. However, a weight programme could help the lead and second gain sweeping strength. Also, sitting leg raises strengthen the quadriceps above the knee and are useful in strengthening the legs for a strong drive out of the hack during the delivery.

Mind games Play mind games like backgammon and memory games that require strategy and concentration.

Practicing

To win, you've got to be dedicated to improvement, and improvement only comes through practice. There's no short cut; anything worthwhile has its price.

A game is half won in practice and preparation, whether on or off the

ice. In any year and in any bonspiel, many teams are equal at the start, but the team that shows the most improvement is the team that wins. The key to success is constant striving for improvement. Evaluate all your games, victories and defeats, and practice, practice, practice.

Practice sessions should last about half an hour, with two sessions a day. Fatigue may set in if you throw too many stones at one time, and this can lead to a bad knee or to bad habits in the delivery. Before both practices and games, warm up. Do stretches to loosen up, and do several slides before actually throwing any stones.

Following are several practice drills that should prove helpful.

Singles Practice draws first; this will help you learn to assess the weight quickly. Pick out an imaginary target and then concentrate on that target with your eye, just as in a game. Alway have a specific shot in mind. Play a game against yourself by alternately throwing opposing stones.

Doubles Play a game of one on one. Try a draw game with light hits permitted. If your entire team is there, two on two is fun and great practice.

Sweeping If all players are in attendance, this is an opportunity to work on your sweeping system. Discuss the call words that will be used to direct the sweep. Then throw shots, just as you would in a game. The skip or third will hold the brush, one player will throw, and two will sweep. Games can be won on calling and sweeping, so take the time to improve.

Shots to practice When practicing takeouts, cover the rings from one side to the other. Master the art of hitting anywhere in the house. You don't want to have a weakness in one particular spot; it could cost you a game.

The least practiced skill is peeling guards. So, when the whole team is present, practice it. If you can peel guards successfully, you will have no trouble making takeouts.

Practice coming around guards and taking stones out with hack weight. Come as close as possible to the guards without wicking. This is a good measuring stick for your players. If they can play hack weight tap-outs around guards and make ninety percent of them, you will be very tough to beat in a game.

At the end of a practice, throw four or five hard takeouts to get the timing of a fast shot. Such a shot may be required in a game, and when it is, you'll be more confident if you've practiced it.

Delivery The main thing to work on in practicing your delivery is accuracy in hitting the brush. Weight will vary from club to club, but hitting the brush is just a straight delivery skill.

When practicing your delivery or when trying to iron out a problem in it, have a friend hold the broom just beyond the first hog line. The stone will not curl at all in that short distance, so your stone should actually strike dead on the broom if thrown properly. If the centre of the stone misses the broom by a few inches, that is the equivalent of a six-inch or one-foot miss at the far end of the ice. Have your friend be your analyst.

Work also at consistency in your delivery. Every move in the delivery — releasing the stone, for example — should be the same every time you perform it. Consistency not only helps the person throwing the stone but also helps the skip, who has to judge how much ice to give on the shot.

Trouble-shooting the delivery Most curlers experience a period when they simply can't slide out straight at the brush. Something is wrong with their delivery; often it takes weeks to find the problem. Here are some suggestions:

Lining up straight When you sit in the hack in the address position, it is very important to line up straight. If you line up improperly, your back-swing will likely be off line and so will your downswing and slide. You will therefore have extreme difficulty in hitting the brush accurately. So, let's go over the correct way to line up in the hack.

Step 1. Set the foot in the hack so the toe points directly at the brush, as in Figure 42. Be

FIGURE 42

A

B

C

FIGURE 43

very exact: The foot may pivot as much as an inch either way to home in on the broom.

Step 2. As you settle down in the hack, look straight at the broom. this will place your head and shoulders square to the broom. Extend the

MHN

right arm fully yet comfortably. Point the outside of the right knee directly at the stone in your hand.

Position the stone Many curlers start the address position with the stone in a position that seems comfortable but is not on line. Do not use the centre line as a guide. Imagine that a line runs from the target to the centre point between the two hacks and bisects the stone as in Figure 43. If the stone is at all off this line, the aim will be off, the backswing crooked, the slide slightly off target, and the release will angle rather than run directly at the broom.

Have a partner hold the broom at the first hog line and tell you if the stone is on line and if your backswing and downswing are straight on line. A simple adjustment of the stone at address can make all the difference in your swing. Remember, the stone should always be positioned in front of the shoulder.

Timing Often the slide is not straight because of poor timing or rhythm. Your body should not lead the downswing; rather, your body should follow the stone. This can be accomplished by slowing down or pausing at the top of the backswing before starting the downswing. Finish the backswing first; this will produce the ideal position to lead into the downswing. The left shoulder should never be lower than the right shoulder or lead the right shoulder. If it does, the right arm will bend unintentionally and the stone will not lead as it should.

The handle In the swing, the stone should remain exactly as it was during the address. The turn of the handle should not change in either direction during the backswing. If the handle turns, the swing will be crooked and the stone will not return to the same position as at address. Don't let your hand rotate the stone until the midpoint of the slide, at which time you can begin to turn the handle in preparation for the release.

Exactly how you set your turns in the stance is a matter of personal preference. Some people start their in turn at eleven o'clock, others at twelve o'clock, others at one o'clock. Likewise, out-turns can be started from three o'clock to twelve o'clock.

Checkpoints for practice:
1. Check the position of the handle at the address.
2. Check the position of the handle at the top of the backswing.
3. Check the position of the handle in the first three feet of the slide.
For a good swing, the handle should be in the same position at all three points.

The rudder leg During the slide, the trailing leg should be straight behind the body. You can check this on fresh pebble. Slide at the broom; then come back behind the hack and see the

sliding mark made in the ice by the dragging leg. It should be straight toward the target, with no fish-tailing.

The sliding foot Problems with delivery are often the result of the sliding foot not coming out exactly at the broom. If the sliding foot is not positioned properly behind the stone, the slide will drift, and so will the stone after the release.

Practice sliding, without a stone, at a target. Concentrate on getting the sliding foot moving directly at the target.

The head Keep the head as still as possible during the swing. Moving the head from side to side interferes with balance, eye concentration, and mind concentration. Keep the head perfectly still, and your slide will be in the groove.

The grip You need control of the stone, yet you need excellent feel to make finesse shots. On fast shots, take a fuller grip so you have more control of the stone. But with soft finesse shots, grip the stone with your fingers to improve the feel.

The palm of the hand should not touch the handle. The thumb is on

58

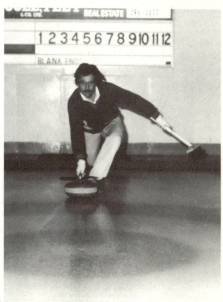

top of the handle or down along the inside of the handle so the point of the "v" between thumb and forefinger aims at the opposite shoulder. The fingers caress the underside of the handle. On extremely keen ice, it is possible to use only the fingertips and still control the stone.

The turn The amount of turn on the stone is something you should work on in practice. The more you spin a stone, the less it will curl and the farther its momentum will carry it (more spin, more energy). A fast-spinning stone is useful for removing guards as you get more action with the shooter, a stronger roll after the hit. However, a slow handle (less than one rotation) curls more, especially at the end, and is particularly efficient in drawing around guards. The slower the handle, the greater is the effect of sweeping on the curl because there is a greater range of curl to play with. Mastering the amount of turn is difficult and it is easy to outsmart yourself, so work on it in practice first.

How low to slide usually, the lower you slide, the better your balance and smoothness. The only drawback to sliding really low is draw weight. Players who stay up a little higher seem to have better draw weight.

Preparing for the Game

Have a set way of getting ready for the game. Too much sleep or too large a meal is not good right before a game, as the brain is then too inactive during the match. Try to be alert and get "hyped up." Think curling and nothing else. You have to be hungry — a little in your stomach and a whole lot in your mind!

Based on what you know of your opposition, try to play the game in your mind before you even step on the ice. This thought process gets your mind ready for problems before they arise and may help you avoid an error. Think over the strengths and weaknesses of your opponent, and map out your game plan.

Be positive in thought and word just before going on the ice. Be as ready as you can be. Warm up properly so you are loose and ready for your first delivery.

As soon as the game starts, get your mind in gear. When you step on the ice, forget the leaky tap at home and the fight with your boss at work; concentrate strictly on the game. Also, concentrate strictly on *your* game. Don't get involved in watching all the other matches. If you want to watch the other games, you should buy a ticket and be a spectator, if you're there to play then play.

Never think ahead to the game after this one. Often players are so worried about the tough team they will play next that they totally forget to win the current game. Don't look ahead.

It is vital to pick the ice up early. Remember, you play the ice as much as you play the opponent. It is you against the course (the ice), and if you have the ice mastered, the opponent is in for a tough time.

There are many ways you can "psych out" the other team. The best way is to exude such confidence that the opposition feel they are only there to lose. And remember, you are there to win.

Reading the Ice

You learn the ice from every shot that travels down the sheet, whether you are delivering team or not.

Memorise where the broom was given; the rings are excellent aids. Observe the release to see if it was wide or narrow. Watch the stone curl down the ice. Did it stay straight or curl early? Did it curl at the end? How much did it curl from release to stopping? What was the weight like? Memorise what occurred. Try to review the ice continually in your mind. If you don't, it is easy to go blank. Curling ice is like a golf green, and you have to master the blueprint. The ice can beat you just as easily as the opposition can, but make the ice your friend and it will help you.

The reading of the ice should start right from the moment you are scheduled on a specific sheet. It is helpful to observe a few ends of a game on the sheet. On tricky ice, shots on a specific sheet are often missed game after game on the same side, the amateur side.

In many clubs, each sheet is a carbon copy of all the others, a certain "type." Try to type the ice as soon as possible; it's a fast way of setting a blueprint of the sheet in your mind.

Your strategy should take into account the type of ice you are playing on and use it to your advantage. Following are several common types and the best strategic ways to use them:

Slanted When you have last rock, play side guards to the lower side of the ice to count points. Play raises on the high side of the ice.

FIGURE 44

Slanted   Bowled

Peaked

61

Bowled It is useless to try to draw around side guards. Only play side guards close to the rings for future raises. Keep the middle open when you have last stone and go for the steals when you don't. Keep your draws high in the rings.

Peaked (The most common type of ice today) Play the corner-guard draw game when you have last stone. Don't be afraid of centre guards, even when you have last stone, as the centre game will be hit and roll behind rather than draw behind. But if you do draw behind centre guards, either bury your stone or leave them just short. Don't set up hit and rolls for the opponent.

In order to learn the specific properties of the ice you're playing on, play both turns in as many new spots as possible with your lead and second shots. With third and skip shots, try to play a turn or spot with which you are familiar. These shots are too late in the end for experimentation.

Try to know the ice better than the opposition does. It will increase your confidence and eliminate nagging doubts in the hack.

It is the skip's job to read the ice, and nothing destroys a team more quickly than a skip who can't read ice. The skip should resist the temptation to run out and sweep. His place is in the rings, judging the shot and learning the ice.

During the game, use the following sequence: observe, learn the lesson, and review. When your opponent throws, find the best position from which to see the stone. Watch for more than just the outcome of the shot; watch the path and movement of the stone.

Remember, the ice will change through the game, so keep on observing and reviewing. On freshly pebbled ice, the rocks will run straight, but they will gradually curl more as the pebble wears down. Takeouts should be thrown firmly in the first two ends, especially corner takeouts, until the ice keens up. Stay alert and exchange information about changing ice conditions as the game progresses.

Learning the Weight

The weight in curling varies from ice rink to ice rink, from sheet to sheet, from end to end, and from spot to spot on the ice. It's important to catch on quickly to the weight early in the game and equally important to adjust to changes in weight as they occur. You learn both skills by playing the game.

The ice is freshly pebbled at the beginning of a game and, therefore, fairly uniform. If you're ready to play, you can get an early sense of the starting weight by watching the first shot of the game on an adjacent sheet. After a few stones have been thrown, trails will start to develop. Keep track of the locations of the trails and of how quickly they keen up with wear.

Here are some general rules about weight:

1. Freshly pebbled ice will be heavy at the beginning but will keen up enough during the game to add fifteen feet to a shot.

2. The more stones and sweepers going down a trail, the keener it will be.

3. Drawing to the rings: A stone will take less time to travel the distance and stop in the rings on heavy ice (the stone is thrown harder and stops faster) than it will on keen ice. Today, many players use a stop watch to time the stone from hog to hog in an attempt to learn the weight. For example, if the average time from hog to hog is twelve seconds for a draw, fourteen seconds indicates keener ice and ten seconds heavier ice.

4. The ice should be uniform weight all over the sheet at the start of the game. The centre lane of the ice will generally keen up more quickly than the outside edges. The centre gets more use, and therefore the pebble wears smoother, allowing the stone to slide faster. However, the keen centre lane should widen as the ends pass, and by the eighth end, the sides of the sheet may be keen as well.

5. The heavier the ice, the more quickly stones will grind to a halt. On keen ice, the stones just seem to keep sliding.

6. A stone that travels in a straight line will not cover as much total distance as a stone that curls considerably. This means that often the keenest path on a sheet is the straight falling turn.

Every member of the team is responsible for learning the weight, but the amount of curl in the ice is the skip's responsibility. The lead and second should concentrate on weight alone; they are the first to test new ice and they also have the responsibility of sweeping.

Here, ideally, is how a lead and second should set about learning the weight.

Tom and Jim (shown in the photograph) are standing at the hog line as the stone passes. They observe the weight thrown at the point of release, watch the stone travel, and see how fast it stops. Tom is checking his stop watch as he times the rock from hog to hog.

The lead and second should also count the stones that go down each spot in the ice in the first two ends of th game (Figure 45). Across tee line A in the diagram are numbers indicating the number of stones thrown on each path in the first end. Path R had the heaviest traffic and should be the keenest. If, on the second end, the skip asks his lead to draw into the rings, he might choose either path S or path T. Path S should have keened up by about ten feet at this stage in the game, but if the skip gives path T, which has not yet been played, the lead will have to throw just as hard as in the first end.

In the first and second ends, observe the exact path of each stone and count the number of shots that travel along each trail in the ice. Keen trails will develop. Heavy trails will remain. Keep track of where the pebble is wearing down.

As the game progresses, you will become more familiar with the ice and your draw weight should improve. Review your own past draw shots regularly to keep track of changes in draw weight. When you prepare to throw a draw, think back on your previous shots. Should this one be a little harder than the last one? A little softer? Did your last shot stop at the back of the house without sweeping? If it did, then you can throw ten feet less weight this time and let the sweepers carry it the rest of the way. Reviewing your past shots every time you go to draw will help you understand your personal feel for the ice and will generally improve your draw weight.

The draw shot is particularly susceptible to human error. If the ice is heavy, ninety percent of the draws that are missed will be short. If the ice is extremely keen, most missed draws will travel too far. It's as if people were made to play close to a norm. When they must play in extreme conditions, they underadjust; they miss on the amateur side.

Here are a couple of examples of extreme conditions and how to adjust to them:

1. The first end: This usually means heavy ice, but most people will underthrow and end up light of the house. Throw the weight you think will carry the rock into the rings with no sweeping. If you rely on sweeping when the ice is heavy, you might pull back slightly on the weight and the shot will be light. You have to throw it where you want it. This takes courage.

2. Keen ice: The danger on keen ice is throwing heavy so the stone slides too far. Always remember that you have a range of about ten feet when you draw on keen ice. If you are going to draw a stone right to the spot where you want it without any sweep, then you had better be very sure of your weight. If you are not completely sure, throw the stone five to ten feet short of the goal and let your sweepers help. Rely on sweeping when the ice is keen.

Decisions

In curling, the responsibility for making decisions rests mainly with the skip. The third can make suggestions

on his own and the skip's shots, while the lead and second should give strategic advice only when called upon. Too many cooks can spoil the broth, especially in curling where every shot is a new decision.

To avoid confusion, set up a decision-making system and stick to it. There are a number of things to decide on most shots: which shot? which turn? what weight? what ice? Since the skip and third consult on many shots, it helps to set out a standard order in which these decisions are made. Here is one system that works well:

1. Select the shot: Ninety percent of the time, the skip's first reaction will determine the shot. If your first reaction isn't very strong, then look at two or three possibilities. Once you have decided, forget about the alternatives.

If the third and skip can't decide, then the lead and second should be invited to comment; often, a team vote is best. Certainly, near the end of the game on a crucial shot the decision should be made by the team as a whole.

If the front end is not pleased with a decision, it is imperative to stop the skip and question him before he gets halfway to the hack. Curling shots should always be decided at the end of the ice where the stones are in play.

Most decision-making discussions occur on the skip's stones. No matter what system the team has developed for making decisions, remember that the skip has to throw the stones and the final choice should be his. He has been watching the ice, and he knows his own strengths and weaknesses. In the final analysis, he should choose the shot he knows he has the best chance of making.

2. Select the turn: Generally, choose the turn that has been played most often in the game.
3. Select the weight: Choose according to individual preference.
4. Select the ice.

Decisions are made in two basic ways — by thinking and by reacting. In curling, thinking means you are unsure of yourself. If you have to think about a shot, then take the time to think hard. The best way to make a decision in a game is by reacting. The subconscious takes over, draws on experience, and flashes you the right answer. It is usually wise to play your first reaction, but take the time to execute it properly.

Holding the Brush

As the skip, always indicate the shot and ice to the player in the hack as soon as you have worked them out. This gives the player time to concen-

The game is not without its funny moments. Here Paul teases Richard Belyea by mimicking his use of the whistle.

trate on the shot while cleaning off the stone. Hold the broom so it is clearly visible right in front of your body, not off to the side. Stand with your feet slightly apart to give the thrower a good view of the broom. Do not move the broom until the thrower has released the stone.

Once the skip has set the broom for his own shot, the third should hold it there until the shot is released. If the third moves away, returns, and puts the broom back down, it may be in a slightly different spot.

Often you will discover in a game that one of your players is regularly missing or shading the broom on one side. Since it is difficult for the player to cure the problem during the game without losing concentration, the skip should simply tell him not to worry and should adjust the broom. Don't try to fix your delivery during a game; leave it to the practice session.

Thinking Before the Delivery

This is the most vital thinking you will do in the game. The goal is to make the shot, and to do this, you will need full concentration. Develop a method of getting mentally set for the delivery.

Relax the nerves You can't make an important shot if you are a bundle of nerves. Slow down a little. It helps to glance away from the broom for a second to relax the eyes before fixing them on the broom.

Remove the doubts Is that the right shot? You should be convinced of it before you get into the hack. Is the ice right? Likely it is. Convince yourself that your best chance is to hit the broom. Don't be afraid to hit the broom. If you try to shade the broom one way or the other, you will cause a lot of your own misses.

Make the shot first Often a curler is so worried about what the opponent might do next that he talks himself right out of the shot, and then he's really in trouble. You have a better chance of dealing with the consequences of their shot if you succeed in making your own shot first.

Thinking after the delivery.

Forget about your delivery Think about your style in practice, but in a game forget your delivery. Let if flow on its own. Put all your mental effort into concentrating on the shot.

One-thought principle People have a difficult time concentrating fully on two things at the same time. Don't try to concentrate both on draw weight and on hitting the broom. On a takeout, first decide the weight to be thrown, then concentrate completely on the broom. On a draw, fix your eyes on the broom — they will hit it for you — and concentrate totally on your feeling for the weight.

Adrenalin Often, on the final shot of a big game, a skip will overthrow. This is caused by the excitement of the moment; the adrenalin is flowing, and the player simply becomes too strong. Cure this problem by recognising it when it occurs. Your blood

will seem to rush and so will you. Take an extra moment to calm yourself, regain your composure, and then play on.

Eye on the Broom

Keep your eye on the broom right through the entire delivery. If you take your eye off the broom for a second, or glance away too soon on a release, you may be causing an error. The name of the game is concentration, and here it is the concentration of the eye on the broom, even after the release.

Pick the bottom of the broom as your focus point, and keep your eye glued there. If you force yourself to maintain that eye concentration even after the release, you'll develop a good follow-through and your shooting will improve.

Releasing the Stone

Aim at a soft finger-tip release. The fingers, which grip the underside of the handle, and the thumb, which rides the upper side of the handle, should feel the release and let the stone slip out at the broom. There should be no superfluous hand action. Don't try to spin or turn the stone toward the broom or to push the stone on release. Simply release it smoothly at the broom when the weight feels right. Some players can successfully push on the release, but they are specialists.

The follow-through of the hand is essential. The photograph below shows excellent form. The hand is staying up off the ice for a time after the release. Also, the hand is finishing straight at the broom and not to the left or right. Too many curlers stop their concentration at the moment of release. They come off the shot and don't go through the shot. Keep the hand and eyes concentrated on the target for at least five feet after the release.

It is very important to release the stone the same way in every delivery.

The right throwing arm does not have to be rigid or straight just before or during the release, but rather comfortable and in a position to afford the greatest possible sensitivity to weight as illustrated. If the arm is bent, the elbow should point down to the ice.

In the long run, consistency in the release will improve your success rate in all shots.

Judging the Stone
The broom holder's point of view

Choose the best position for observing the stone and squat back like a baseball catcher so you can shift slightly from side to side. The slight movement will help your perception. Stay very low and keep your eyes glued to the travelling stone. Stay down on hits; don't move too early to sweep the roll. Dash out quickly if a draw needs help but only if the line of the shot is of no concern. Keep the brush in front of you and pointing at the centre on the oncoming stone. This

CS

MB

will help the sweepers with the line of the shot.

Calling the stone accurately on its journey down the ice can determine the outcome of a game. Use a system. Choose single-word commands and make sure every team member knows them. For example:

Yes Sweep as hard as you can.

No Do not sweep but have your brooms very close at a "ready" position.

Off do not sweep at all; don't even keep the stone clean. The shot needs to curl or slow down a lot.

One The shot is on perfect line. It does not need to be swept hard but should be kept clean so that it does not pick up any debris. One sweeper keeps the stone clear by sweeping very lightly, while the other keeps his head up, watching for new instructions.

Room You are coming past a guard and there is still plenty of space between your shooter and the guard, so sweep only for weight.

Line No matter what the weight, the stone is close to wicking the guard, so sweep to hold it straight. This is an excellent command because it not only tells the sweepers what to do but also tells them why.

It is essential that, before a skip's stone is delivered, the third and skip know exactly which shot is being played. Too often the skip may be calling for a hit and roll one way and the third the other way. That kind of mistake can be expensive. Get together ahead of time.

In calling the sweep, keep the stones that are in play in front of you so you can see everything. Here Rick is called a raise back onto a stone in the rings. He is positioned behind the stone in the rings, calling the sweep and giving the location or line of the stone to the sweepers by keeping his broom on line with the oncoming stone.

The thrower's point of view

Keep your head very close to the ice, so you get the best possible view of the line. If you are low enough, you can see the edge of the stone that you have thrown at exactly the same height as the edge of a stone at the far end. If you are higher than this, your judgement of the stone's line will be less accurate. If you are only concerned with weight on a shot, then get up as soon as the release is complete and stay right behind your stone all the way.

Sweeping

Curling has become an exacting game. You must be able to draw and also to takeout and roll to the inch. This requires precision. In the execution of a shot, delivery is important, but so are sweeping and calling. All three must be good if the shot is to be precise.

Calling Calling works in two directions: The sweepers yell information about the travelling weight to the thrower, and the thrower and skip call for sweeping according to the curl and line of the stone. The calls should be single words which are clearly understood by everyone on the team. Without good calling, you won't have good sweeping.

Sweepers' Duties Before the stone is thrown, clean the path from the hack to the hog line, so the stone cannot pick up debris during the slide. Review the path, determining the exact line the stone will travel. As a sweeper, you instill confidence in the thrower by letting him know his shot is in good hands.

Sweeping duties vary, depending upon the shot. In general, however, the sweeper should react to the person who is calling for the curl or line, call out the weight of the shot as accurately as possible to the person who is judging the curl, and judge the weight of the stone himself, adjusting his sweeping accordingly.

The relative importance of each of the sweepers' duties depend on the shot:

Takeout

1. React to the caller. Reacting quickly is vital.

2. Yell the weight only if it is wrong (heavy, light).

Here a sweeper shows a better-than-average ability to react to the caller!

73

Hack weight

1. React to the caller.

2. Yell the weight if it is wrong at any point down the sheet of ice.

3. Yell the weight when you get to the last hog line, whether it's right or wrong. The caller may want to go for a perfect inside roll but needs to know if there is sufficient weight to tap the stone out of the rings. Use the following cue words:

Heavy Sweep is not needed for the sake of weight.

Light Sweep is needed for the sake of weight.

Lots There is sufficient weight to tap the rock nicely through the rings, so there is a chance to play for a better roll.

Draw weight *(Going around a guard)*

1. Judge the weight for yourself and sweep for weight.

2. Yell the weight to the caller: for example, heavy, tee, front ring, light.

3. React to the call. If the call is "line," there's very little room to the guard, and you should sweep and yell the weight for information. If the call is "room," there is plenty of room to the guard, so whether you sweep depends entirely upon your own judgement of weight.

Draw weight *(An open draw)*

1. Sweep only on your own judgement. Sweepers should be able to judge the weight better than the thrower or the caller.

2. Yell the weight so other members of the team know what you are doing and why. On this kind of draw, the sweeper is in control.

Pointers on sweeping technique

A. While sweeping, make sure your back foot does not block the thrower's view of the rock. He must be able to see all of the moving stone in order to make an accurate call.

B. Keep your head up. Whether sweeping full out, keeping it clean, or not sweeping at all, at least one of the two sweepers should be looking directly at the person holding the broom in order to catch any new command and react to it quickly. If both sweepers have their heads down, the stone may move several feet before the sweepers react to a new command.

C. Too often, an excellent release becomes a missed shot as a result of catching debris on the ice. the sweepers must keep the path clean. With a corn broom, sweep gently in short, quick strokes. With a push broom, keep the brush on the ice, directly in front of the stone, exerting only minimal pressure. Don't sweep hard enough to speed the stone up; simply keep it under control and free of junk.

D. To judge draw weight, glance alternately from the stone to its destination. Watch the rotation of the stone. If a normally turning handle suddenly takes a quick spin, the stone has picked up some junk and you had better sweep.

E. The closer the stone is to the target, the more precise will be your judgement. A stone heading for the button should be eased toward the top of the rings by the sweepers; then extra effort can be applied, if necessary, from the top of the house to the destination. In other words, the sweepers should keep the stone under control, knowing that they can take it that extra distance at the end if they have to.

F. Stay with the stone. Many sweepers will see a stone thrown with too much weight, assume it's "headed for the lunch counter," and leave, only to see the stone grab and stop short. Stay with the stone, no matter how heavy it seems. It's just as easy to stay with the stone as it is to stand there and do nothing. Besides, sweeping at the end of the shot does the most good.

G. The sweepers should be in the ready position for the release, prepared to assess the weight of the stone as soon as it leaves the thrower's hand.

H. Sweeping corners: You can make a rock curl a little more or a little less just by sweeping more on one edge of the rock than the other, especially if you use a push broom.

A curling stone in motion has an inside edge and an outside edge. The

FIGURE 46

Outside edge

Turn

Direction

Inside edge

inside edge is the side of the cup closest to and the outside edge is the side of the cup fartherst from the direction in which the stone is curling. Figure 46 will help explain:

Look at the stone from above and pretend all you can see is the cup in contact with the ice. Now note the direction the stone is travelling, the turn on the stone, the inside edge, and the outside edge.

If the stone is swept only on the outside edge, it will curl more than if both edges are swept. Sweeping reduces the friction in front of the outside edge, leaving the inside edge to pivot, in turn causing the stone to curl more in that direction. Sweep the outside edge on a draw, at the very end of the shot when the rock digs in.

If the stone is swept only on the inside edge, it will travel straighter. The friction on the outside edge will be slightly greater than on the swept inside edge. As a result, the stone will grab slightly on the outside and counteract the curl. Sweep on the inside edge to hold takeouts straighter and to get by guards.

However, don't expect too much from sweeping corners. The effect of sweeping only one edge is really very slight, and if you don't use the technique at all, you won't be losing any great advantage.

1. Sweeping guards: Sweeping is especially important in trying to keep the line of a guard perfect. Here are a couple of ideas for controlling the line:

If the guard is beginning to over-curl at centre ice, hold the stone straight by sweeping all the way. Early sweeping holds the stone straighter.

When the stone is stopping and is on line, rather than quitting sweeping completely, sweep very lightly — not to alter the weight or line but rather to keep the stone from catching debris and curling suddenly.

VS

MB

Relative advantages of the corn broom and push broom

Corn Broom by Rick Folk

1. Better for spectators; there is a lot of action in straw broom sweeping.

2. They are very effective if used properly.

3. They keep the curler in strong physical shape, especially the forearms, biceps, and triceps.

4. If stones pick up mulch from a straw broom, they will only slow down a bit. A hair from a brush will ruin the movement of a stone entirely.

5. Because straw places mulch on the ice, other teams must sweep very carefully against you.

6. Stones will curl more with mulch on the ice, making it easier to draw behind guards.

7. Corn broom sweeping, I believe, will make takeout shots run straighter. Because the sweepers are not bent over when sweeping (as most push broomers are), their balance is better, they can move faster, and they still sweep with a lot of force.

8. It is easier for broom sweepers to judge the line of the stone as well as the weight because they are more upright and have a better overall view of the shot.

9. When sliding, the corn broom flexes more, which can be better for balance. It is also easier to clean the bottom of the stone with a corn broom.

10. A corn broom will remove debris

from the ice very readily. Because most of the debris is corn mulch, the straws in the broom will "cut" the debris out of the ice more easily.

11. Corn brooms are available in different weights, straw lengths, and designs. There should be a straw broom available for any sweeping technique.

Push Broom by Paul Gowsell

1. Less expensive because they last for a year or two, whereas a straw broom may last only five games.

2. Not so strenous. You can sweep three games a day without getting as tired as you would with a broom. This leaves you fresher for throwing.

3. You can sweep around guards without lifting your brush.

4. They are very effective if used with fast or powerful strokes.

5. You can sweep right up to the boards on a rollout or right up to another stone for a freeze.

6. In the rings, you can sweep in tight areas where there is very little room between stones.

7. If you turn the brush upside down during the slide, there is almost no friction.

8. You can sweep half the cup of the stone with a brush.

9. If you keep the brush down on the path in front of the stone, you can keep the stone perfectly clean.

Use the Other Team's Weaknesses

Take whatever advantage you can. If the other team has a weakness, exploit it to gain points. If the other team has a reputation as a hitting team or a draw team, fit that bit of knowledge into your strategy. If they are young, they will probably be strong hitters but may not yet have mastered the finer points of a draw finesse game. So play a lot of draws against them if drawing is your strength. Always try to play your strength, unless the opposition is even stronger in that area.

If your opponents play the same turn almost all the time, it probably indicates a lack of confidence in the other turn. Go around guards and force them to follow you on their weak turn.

Often you can pick out a weakness by closely watching a player's release. If the release is turned in or flipped out, then the stone will not curl naturally, so force the opponent into that turn.

Always try to determine if the opposing skip is strong at draw or takeout. This will help you to decide if you should force him to draw or hit on his last stone when you have the advantage.

Strategy
Forcing the Side Draw Game

In top-notch curling, sometimes you just can't wait for the other team to miss. You have to build your own offence.

Figure 47: You have the last stone and want two points. The opposition has drawn their first stone, A, into the house. You can take A out and hope the opposition will miss a wide open takeout, or you can go on the offensive.

Ignore A and play a side guard B. Now, whatever the opponent does, you will try to hit their stone and roll behind guard B. Often in this situation, after a few exchanges in the rings and a rollout by the other team, you will have an opportunity to draw behind guard B and force the opponent into a tough shot.

Rather than waiting for an open miss, you are now trying to manufacture two points.

Defending Against the Side Draw Game

There are two main defences against the side (corner guard) draw game:
1. Peel — Remove the side guards and roll away with your shooter.
2. Play a centre guard — Force the opponent to remove the centre guard or gamble with a centre guard draw game.

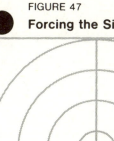

FIGURE 47
Forcing the Side Draw Game

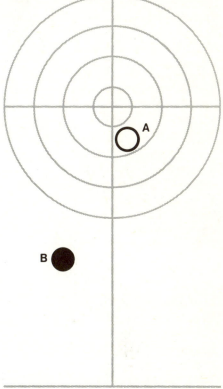

Going for the "Gusto"

The conventional wisdom in curling strategy is to remove centre guards when you have last stone in order to keep the middle open for the hammer. However, sometimes you have to throw safety to the winds and go for the big end that might break a game wide open.

Figure 48: The opponent is placing centre guards. You decide to go for it, the big end. Draw behind guard A to force the issue. If the opponent misses entirely or splits guard A for two side guards, you have a good setup. Once you have control of the end, play freezes and tap-backs to

FIGURE 48

Going for the Gusto

off until your third's last stone. Now you have three stones to come, while they have only two. The odds are in your favour and this is your chance to go for points.

Position Your Shots Properly

Once you are involved in top-flight curling, it is imperative to postion stones properly. Don't be satisfied with simply getting your shot into the rings or somewhere in the general

keep your stones in the rings as counters.

This type of end is good strategy in the middle of a game as an attempt to score a big end.

Be patient

Patience is a virtue. There's always a temptation to try to score a lot of points early and put the game out of reach. To do that, you have to take chances, sometimes too many.

Be patient. Wait for your chance. When the odds are in your favour, then go after it.

For example, if the opponent is putting guards out in front, peel them

FIGURE 49 **Position Rocks Properly**   FIGURE 50 **Combinations**

vicinity of the desired location. Attempt to leave the opponent a tough shot or angle.

Figure 49: If you have a stone A behind the tee and you want to split the rings, the best position for the next stone is also behind the tee (B). Position B1, on the tee line, would not be good because the opponent can hit half of B1 and double out A. Position B2 to A is sharp and the opponent will have to aim for only a small piece of B2.

Combinations

Combination raises are great when they work, but you have to very sure of the angles.

Figure 50: It appears that if you strike the opposition stone A on the right, your stone B will be raised and will remove the shot stone C. However, the angle is often deceptive and the stones may follow the dotted line instead. If the shooter were travelling along line 1, it would drive the stone along the desired line, but because the shooter travels along line 2 and the stones are only half frozen, the stone will not continue along either line 1 or line 2 but will follow a vector between the two, represented by the dotted line.

In Turn or Out Turn?

Figure 51: There are two guards, A and B. You want to draw around stone

81

FIGURE 51 **Play It Safe**

FIGURE 52 **Which Way?**

In turn   Out turn

A, but which turn should you use? Remember, it's not only what you make, but also what you leave. Draw around guard A on the in-turn. If the opposition can see part of your stone, they can take it out, but they will probably roll into the open. Stones in the open are much easier to take out than stones behind guards. If you had played the out-turn and left part of your stone exposed, then they could have taken you out and possibly rolled behind guard B. You would have done them a favour.

Figure 52: Guard A is on the centre line and the opponent's stone B is off centre at the back of the rings. Draw around to give the opponent the greatest degree of difficulty. Play the

in-turn draw. He will have to try to take your stone out, but the angle you have left him is tough because he may hit your stone back on his own.

When deciding which way to draw, there are other factors to consider apart from what you will leave for your opponent. Look at which turn is curling more and which turn your shooter is most comfortable throwing, as well as which turn you want your opponent to throw. Play your strength against their weakness if at all possible.

Force the draw shot on the first end.

Try to make the opposition hit with more of their shots in the early ends

82

○ FIGURE 53
Force the Draw on the First End

○ FIGURE 54
Hold the Opponent to One

Guard

so they won't catch on to draw weight. However, make the opposing skip draw on his last stone when he doesn't yet have his weight.

Figure 53: The opponent has last stone on the first end. You are lying one and throwing your last stone. You can either guard A or draw to the other side. You should guard A, trying to bite the rings. This will force the opponent to draw.

Play it smart. Give up one point.

Sometimes it is wiser to give up one rather than gamble and open it up.

Figure 54: The opponent has last stone. He is shot stone (A), but you

could possibly come through the port and take him out. Is it worth the risk? You might open it up more and give him an easy shot for two. If you aren't desperate to score, it is best to guard with your last stone and simply give the opponent one point.

Second Last End

1. Gain the advantage for the last end if the score is tied.

2. Go for points if possible.

3. If you have last stone and cannot get more than one point, try to blank the end (A). The advantage of last stone is important at this stage.

4. If your opponent has last stone, try to steal or force him to take only

D

one point. Going into the final end down one with last stone is as good as going in one up without last stone.

5. If you do not have last stone, play guards in front of the rings on the centre line (B) to force your opponent. If your opponent tries to remove a guard but hits and stays (C), then draw behind the remaining guard to force the issue (D).

One Up Without, Going Home

One up without the hammer, going home, is not an enviable position. One mistake can result in two points for your opponent, with the game over and no chance of getting back. How should you play it?

FIGURE 55
Second Last End

Score — Even

Most teams play a hitting game to hold the opponent to one point. The opponent plays side guards or freezes to set up the two-ender. If you play the hitting style, you had better be accurate and successful. Try to roll out on all your shots. Leaving too many of your own stones around will cause you problems when you try to remove their counters.

The best bet, the percentage play, is to go for the steal in this situation. Play guards on the centre line. If the opponent peels the guard, play three or four of them and then change to a hitting game. The opponent is keeping it clean for you. If the opponent

draws behind your guard, follow him and play for second shot frozen to his. Keep him from getting that second counter. If you have either first or second shot close to the button guard it.

Last End

1. If you have last stone and the score is tied, play the hitting game. Hit all guards and roll to the sides (A). Keep the centre open for your last shot to win.

2. If you don't have last stone, you are forced to go for the steal. Start by playing centre guards (B) rather than shots into the rings; it is easier for them to take your shot out of the rings than to remove a guard and roll to the side. Once you have a guard in position, draw behind it.

3. When your opponent hits and stays on a guard near the centre line (C), draw behind the guard as close as possible to the button (D).

4. Try to leave the opposing skip as dificult a shot as possible for his last shot.

Going for Three

If you are three points down coming home, here is a good strategy. It is called setting up the goal posts (two corner guards) and kicking the field goal (three points).

Step 1 Play side guard A.
You hope the opponent will nose it. When he does, don't draw around yet.

Step 2 Play another side guard B.
You hope the opponent will nose it. When he does, you have your goal posts.

Step 3 Bury behind guard A with 1.
The opposition, being three up, will play safe and remove guard A to open it up.

Step 4 Draw around guard B with 2.
The opposition will hit 1.

Step 5 Draw around guard B again with 3.
The opponent now has a difficult shot and must try to follow you around guard B.

Step 6 If you get even half a break, you will have a draw or hit for three points.

FIGURE 56
Last End

Score — Even

FIGURE 57
Kicking the Field Goal

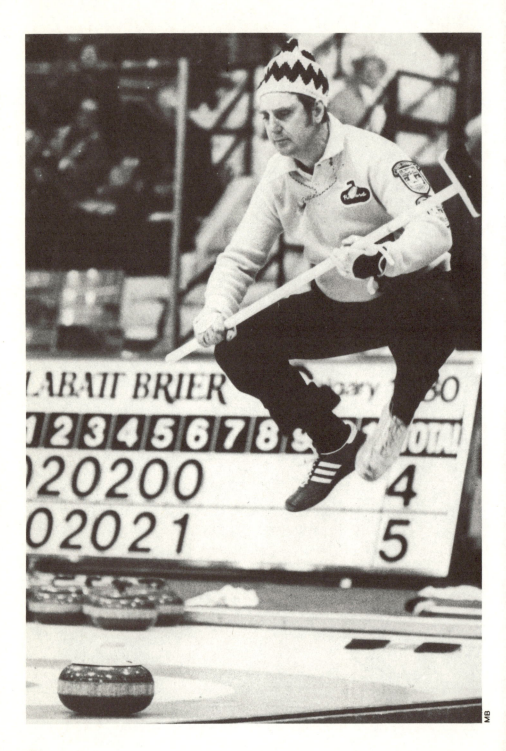

The Pro Side

In curling, every time a stone is thrown, there is a pro side and amateur side to the shot. Here is a list of shots, their circumstance, and their pro or amateur side.

Shot	Circumstances	Pro	Amateur
Takeout	Keen straight ice	Does not miss wide. Uses the sweepers.	Throws it wide, into space. Nothing can help it curl.
Takeout	Very swingy ice	Does not miss inside. Aims for outside $2/3$ of stone.	Throws inside and starts the stone curling.
Draw	Keen ice	Throws to the front ring. Uses the sweepers.	Aims for the tee line, is a little heavy; nothing can help now.
Draw	Heavy ice (first end)	Throws correct weight with no sweep.	Doesn't believe how heavy it is. Throws light. Yells sweep but it doesn't help.
Draw around guard	Straw all over the ice	Does not panic if stone is little heavy or wide. Keeps sweepers cleaning.	Panics if the stone is wide or heavy, yells off to the sweepers at centre ice. Stone grabs debris and is lost.
Draw to a stone behind a guard.	Stone is buried behind guard.	Makes shot or just short for second shot. Can tap it up.	Makes shot or slides too far, all or nothing.
Hack weight around it guard to remove counter	Stone is partly exposed.	Makes shot or removes guard to open it up.	Makes shot or misses entirely, not even removing the guard. Still has same problem left.
Splitting the house	A. You have the advantage of last stone.	In the house or short of the house.	Heavy and loses the opportunity for a side guard.
	B. Opponent has the advantage of last stone.	Not short of the rings.	Falls short, providing a side guard for the opposition.
Hack weight	Tricky hack weight shot.	Throws slightly more than draw weight.	Tries to throw less than takeout weight, which is inaccurate.

Winning

Is winning everything? To many people, it is the only thing that counts. To a winning team, it must certainly be important.

The desire to win is vital to successful curling. So are sacrifice and dedication. Whenever you win something in life, you lose something as well. The curler who wins the championship sacrifices his goal by achieving it. The champion loses his right to play the game as an average curler; regardless of how important the game is to the champion, it is extremely important to the challenger who wants to beat him. Sacrifice goes hand in hand with dedication. To win, you must achieve excellence. And to achieve excellence, you must be dedicated to the game, to work, to practice, to more practice — and that involves a sacrifice of time and energy. Winning is neither easy nor painless, but it is rewarding.

While there are no sure-fire recipes for success, there are certain ingredients you will find in most winning teams:

1. Team members love to play and they love to win. Enthusiasm makes the difference.

2. They pursue quality. To achieve quality they practice; they sacrifice time to improve.

3. They play as a team. Each player thinks more of the team's success than of his own success.

4. They don't blame one another for mistakes. Mistakes can be ironed out in practice. When a mistake is made, they forget it immediately and put their energy into the next shot.

5. Each team member tries to be the best player possible at his position. He's not waiting to be promoted or to replace another team member.

6. Team members believe in one another. Hero worship takes a team a long way.

7. They go the distance; they concentrate for the full 2½ or 3 hours of a game. And they play all out, start to finish, no matter what the score is.

8. Their goal is to win, not to humiliate the opposition.

9. They learn from losing. They improve with winning.

10. They don't let a run of bad luck get them down. They don't use excuses. They feel that if they are good enough, they can defeat both the other team and luck as well.

11. Their drive or determination is tremendous. They feel they can win and nothing can stop them.

12. They are fortunate if their personal lives don't interfere with their curling. If their personal problems are of such gravity that they interfere with concentration during a game, then the curling will suffer.

13. To develop a championship team, the practice and the skills must become routine. That's what it's all about — just routine.

Section 4
Champions

History of World Curling Championship Competition

1959 Ernie Richardson of Canada wins the first world championship ever held by defeating Scottish champion Willie Young in a five-game series (the Scotch Cup).

1961 The United States enters world competition followed by Sweden in 1962, Switzerland and Norway in 1964, France in 1968, and Germany in 1967.

1966 The International Curling Federation (ICF), curling's governing body, is formed.

1968 The World Championship becomes known as the Air Canada Silver Broom.

1973 Italy and Denmark are admitted to international competition. The Canadian Curling Hall of Fame is instituted.

1975 The first World Uniroyal Junior Men's Championship is held.

1979 The first World Ladies' Curling Championship is held.

Curling Legends

Graeme Adam

Hutcheson's Boys Grammar School was instrumental in introducing Graeme Adam to curling in 1967. Only two years later, with Brian Alderman at third, Graeme won the Scottish National Schools Championships, and repeated his success the following season. That same year with the young Ken Horton in his team he won the RCCC Rink Championship. Still playing Brian at third, over the next few years, Graeme's rink was a force to be

reckoned with and he was successful in many competitions; Benson & Hedges (four wins between 1975 and 1980), Stranraer Mediterranean Cruise 1975/76 and 1977/78. With Ken Horton playing third in 1980/81 he won the Ayr International and for the last two years the Edinburgh International trophy has been in the custody of the Adam rink.

Peter Attinger — *Switzerland*

Peter Attinger has represented Switzerland in two world Championships — 1974 and 1979. He lost a last-stone final game to Kristian Soerum of Norway in 1979.

Pierre Boan — *France*

Pierre Boan of the Mont D'Arbois Curling Club has been France's perennial representative in the Silver Broom. Boan has represented France eleven times in the Silver Broom and has always made an impression as a

very colourful participant. He won the French championship from 1968 to 1978 inclusive.

91

Norman Brown

Norman was only 9 years old when he started curling in the newly opened Stranraer Ice Rink where he also attended Saturday morning instruction classes. Later, whilst a pupil at George Watson's College he was coached by Chuck Hay at Perth. In his last year at school Norman won the Scottish National Schools Championships. In 1980 he played

third to Andrew McQuistin when McQuistin's team won the World Junior Championship and finished runners-up in the Scottish Championship. Norman will always be remembered for his magnificent triple take-out in that World Junior final in Kitchener, Ontario in 1980, which helped win the game for Scotland.

Kerry Burtnyk — *Winnipeg, Manitoba*

At the age of only twenty-two, Kerry Burtnyk won the 1981 Brier and

became the youngest skip ever to accomplish the feat. To win the championship, Burtnyk pulled off the most stunning reversal of fortunes in the history of the Brier. He scored three on the last end of the final playoff game to defeat Allan Hackner from Thunder Bay 5-4. Burtnyk also was the number one money winner during the 1980-81 season. His 1981 Canadian champions were third Mark Olson, second Jim Spencer, and lead Ron Kammerlock.

Don Duguid — *Winnipeg, Manitoba*

Don "Dugie" Duguid is familiar to curling fans as a record-breaking champion, as well as a colourful commentator with the CBC on major curling event coverage. Duguid is a three-time Brier winner. He played third for Terry Braunstein in 1965 and skipped his team of third Ron Hunter, second Jim Pettapiece, and lead Bryan Wood to both the Brier and World championships in 1970 and '71. Now retired, he holds a record of seventeen straight wins in world championship events, playing undefeated in the 1970 and '71 seasons. Duguid and his team be-

came members of the Curling Hall of Fame in 1974.

Otto Danielli — *Switzerland*
Until Jurg Tanner's victory in 1981, Otto Danielli was the only Swiss skip ever to have won the Silver Broom. Danielli took the title in 1975, defeating Ed Risling of the U.S.A. Playing with Danielli were third Roland Schneider, second Rolf Gautchi, and lead Ueli Mulli. Danielli is now coaching curling at the national competitive level.

Hector Gervais — *St. Albert, Alberta*
Hec Gervais has earned many of curling's top honours, including two Brier titles and a World Championship. He skipped four Brier entries, placing second in 1962 and 1970, winning in 1961 and 1974, and following his 1961 win with the World Championship title. The "Friendly Giant" is known for his unbeatable

push shot and during his curling career represented Northern Alberta nine times in provincial curling play-downs. Gervais was inducted into the Curling Hall of Fame in 1975.

Soren Grahm
Soren Grahm (Sweden) shot to fame in March 1982 when he won the World Junior Championship in Fredericton, New Brunswick, without the loss of a single game — 9 wins in the round-robin and a final victory over Canada's Mert Thompsett, a feat never before accomplished. Two weeks later in Garmisch at the Silver

93

Broom, Soren skipped a different team to the semi-final only just losing out to Canada's brilliantly consistent Al Hackner who went on to win the following day.

Allan Hackner — *Thunder Bay, Ontario*

Allan Hackner was the runner-up in the Brier in 1980 and 1981. He first appeared on the national scene in the 1980 Brier played in Calgary. He surprised many when he defeated Paul Gowsell in the semi-final and then lost to Rick Folk in the final. Hackner finished in the first place in the 1981 Brier and then lost the most unbelievable final in Brier history. Up two in Kerry Burtnyk going into the last end, he lost 5-4 after giving up

a three-ender. Hackner is nicknamed "The Iceman" because he is cool and unflappable under pressure, which helped him win the Silver Broom in 1982.

Colin Hamilton

Colin started curling at Haymarket Ice Rink at the age of 9, and entered his first competition when only 14. His first major success was in the Scottish Junior Championship in 1977/78 when he also competed in the World Junior Championships in Switzerland. Playing out of Gogar Park, Colin with his new team of Mike Dick, David Ramsay and Richard Prestel won the Edinburgh International in 1980/81. He rounded off this extremely successful season

with wins in the Inverness Invitation and the Scottish Championships which led to representing Scotland in the Silver Broom. The next season also started well with the team winning the Perth Masters and retaining their title as Scottish champions. On the international front Colin represented Scotland in 1981/82 in the European Championships and in the Silver Broom in Garmisch.

Chuck Hay — *Scotland*
Chuck Hay skipped the only team from Scotland ever to win the World Curling Championship. Appropriately, Hay and his team won the competition in Perth in 1967, the last year that the Scotch Whisky Association sponsored the championship. Playing with him on the winning team were third John Bryden, second Alan

Glen, and lead David Howie. Hay lost the world title to Ron Northcott of Canada in 1968, the first year of Air Canada's sponsorship of the Silver Broom. Hay is now Scotland's National Coach.

Elizabeth Hogstrom — *Karlstad, Sweden*
Elizabeth Hogstrom lost the final game of the World Ladies' Championship in 1980 to Canada's Marj Mitchell. In 1981 Hogstrom won the competition, defeating Susan Seitz of

Canada for the world ladies title. Playing with her on the championship team were third Carina Olsson, second Birgitta Sewik, and lead Karin Sjogren. In 1982 she lost in the final in Geneva to Marianne Jörgensen.

Ken Horton
Following in the footsteps of brothers Bill and David, who have 8 Scottish Junior titles between them, Ken started curling at Crossmyloof in Glasgow. His first major success came after four years when at the age of 14 he was a member of Graeme Adam's team which won the R.C.C.C. Rink Championship. Following a series of junior successes, Ken formed his own team with Willie Jamieson, Keith Douglas and Richard Harding which won the Scottish Championship in 1977 and went on to represent Scotland at the Silver Broom in Karlstad, Sweden where they reached the semi-finals (the last Scottish team to do so). Ken has continued to build up an impressive

95

McKee three more times — 1971, '72, and '73 — as the second on the team skipped by Vera Pezer, bringing McKee's total wins to six, a record unequalled by any other curler in Canada. She has won numerous regional competitions, participated in the Carling O'Keefe Super League and the 1954 British Empire Games in Vancouver, and been named Saskatoon's sportswoman of the year in 1969. Still active in curling at an administrative and competitive level. McKee curls out of the Nutana Club in Saskatoon.

list of successes and there is no doubt that we will see him add to it over the next few years.

Joyce McKee — *Saskatoon, Saskatchewan*

Joyce McKee, the queen of ladies, curling, was one of the first women to use the long sliding delivery. She skipped her first Canadian Ladies' Championship (formerly called the Lassie) in 1960. At that time the championship match was played between the best teams from the east and west. The first ten-province competition for women was in 1961, and McKee's team claimed top place. She skipped the winning team for a third time in 1969, with Vera Pezer playing third. The Canadian Ladies' Championship title belonged to

Andrew McQuistin

Andrew McQuistin started curling in 1970 at Stranraer Ice Rink. His first major competition was in 1975 when he played third to Peter Wilson in the World Junior Championships at Toronto, with Neale McQuistin at second and John Sharp lead. The team won the bronze medal after losing to Sweden in the semi-finals. However, in 1976 the same team won the Bill Ross Trophy in Sweden. In the final of the World Junior Championships in 1979 with Andrew as skip, Neale McQuistin (third), Hugh Aitken (second) and Dick Adams (lead) they were squeezed into second place by the U.S.A. 1980, however, saw victory for the young Scots team when they defeated Canada's Mert Thompsett in the final.

Bill Muirhead — *Perth, Scotland*
A competitive curler since 1965, Bill Muirhead of Scotland has been his country's representative in the Silver Broom three times. Curling out of the St. Martins club in Perth, he played in

the Air Canada championship in 1969, 1970, and 1976 — the last Scottish team to reach the final.

Bobby Nichols — *United States*
Bobby Nichols first appeared on the world curling scene in 1974 in Berne, when he played third on Bud Somerville's winning Silver Broom team. Nichols skipped the winning U.S.A. team in the 1978 Silver Broom, playing with third Bill Strum, second Tom Locken, and lead Bob Christman. In 1981 Nichols again combined with Somerville, and they made it to the

final of the Silver Broom with Somerville skipping and throwing third stones and Nichols throwing last stone.

Bob Pickering — *Milestone, Saskatchewan*
There is no more distinguished "bridesmaid" in the history of the Brier than Bob "Peewee" Pickering. Six times (five as skip), he represented Saskatchewan in the Brier, but he was never able to get his hands on the Brier tankard. His team primarily was comprised of third Garnet Campbell, second Jack Keyes, and lead Gary Ford. Pickering is most noted for having the highest backswing in

curling. Now semi-retired from competitive curling, Bob Pickering is a Member of the Legislative Assembly in Saskatchewan.

Ernie Richardson — *Regina, Saskatchewan*

Ernie Richardson is known as "The King"; he skipped the only team to win four World Championships and four Canadian briers. The Richardson team was named the all-star team for the first fifty years of the Brier, and Ernie Richardson and Arnold Richardson were named all-star skip and third respectively. Second, Sam Richardson the heart of the team, was selected runner up as the best second for the first fifty years of the Brier. Wes Richardson was the lead for their first three World Championships

while Mel Perry was their lead in 1963. The entire team has been elected to the Curling Hall of Fame.

Jim Sanderson

Jim was first introduced to curling in 1958 at the age of 12, and has hardly been off the ice since. His international career peaked in 1971, when he represented Scotland in the Silver broom at Megere where he was narrowly defeated in the final by Don Duguid of Canada, and 1978 again in the Silver Broom he was squeezed out by Kristian Sorum of Norway. Jim has played in six Scottish Championships winning in 1971 and 1978, and semi-finalist in 1973 and 1979. He has been a consistent competitor and also won

Kristian Soerum — *Oslo, Norway*
Kristian Soerum first appeared on the world curling scene as Norway's representative in the 1976 Silver Broom. Since then, he has represented Norway every year and was the Silver Broom Champion in 1979.

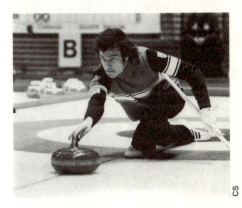

CS

the Scottish Mixed Championships in 1978, and the National Pairs in 1980.

Susan Seitz — *Calgary, Alberta*
Susan Seitz won the 1981 Canadian Ladies' Curling Championship. The event was played that year in St. John's Newfoundland. Sharing the title were third Judy Erickson, second Myrna McKay, and lead Betty Mc-Cracken. In a final playoff for the world title, she was defeated by Elizabeth Hogstrom of Sweden.

He was the Silver Broom runner-up in 1978 and 1980. The members of his team in 1979 were third Morten Soerum, second Eigil Ramsfjell, and lead Gunnar Meland.

Bud Somerville — *United States*
Bud Somerville is the most outstanding curler from the U.S.A. in its world curling history. When Somerville won his first World Curling Championship in 1965, he became the first non-Canadian to take the title. The other

team members were third Bill Strum, second Al Gagne, and lead Tom Wright. He also skipped the U.S.A.'s entry in the 1968 and '69 Silver Brooms and again won the world competition in 1974 in Berne, Switzerland, with third Bob Nichols, sec-

MB

ond Bill Strum, and lead Tom Locken. Somerville was sidelined in 1978 with open heart surgery but returned to the Silver Broom in 1981. The American team made it to the final with Somerville skipping and throwing third stones and third Bob Nichols throwing last stone.

Jurg Tanner — *Lusanne, Switzerland*

Jurg Tanner is the 1981 Silver Broom champion. Playing with third Jurg Hornisberger, second Patrik Loertscher, and lead Franz Tanner, he defeated Bud Somerville of the U.S.A. in the final. Tanner's team also represented Switzerland in the 1980 Silver Broom played in Moncton and in 1982 at Garmisch, Germany.

Mert Thompsett — *Winnipeg, Manitoba*

In 1979, Mert Thompsett won Manitoba's first Canadian Junior Curling crown, playing with third Lyle Derry, second Joel Gagne, and lead Mike Friessen. Thompsett lost the title in

1980 but came back to win again in 1981 with third Bill McTavish, second Joe Gagne, and lead Mike Friessen. The team represented Canada in the World Junior competition in March, 1982, losing in the final to Sweden's Soren Grahn.

Alex F. Torrance

Alex first represented Scotland in 1964 in the Scotch Cup held at Calgary in Canada when they were narrowly defeated after an extra end by Lyall

Dagg of Canada. In 1972 Alex again played for his country in the Silver Broom at Garmisch in Bavaria. The Scottish Champions reached the semi-finals only to be pipped once again by the Canadians. With a slightly changed team of Alex F. Torrance, Alex Torrance, Bill Kerr and Tom McGregor, Alex again represented Scotland in the 1973 Silver Broom. However the Canadians proved to be the jinx of the Scots team, beating them in the semi-final after an extra end. Alex's last appearance in the Silver Broom was at Perth in 1975, although on that occasion he failed to reach the semi-finals.

Jim Waddell

Jim's first major international year was in 1964 when, playing lead to Alex F. torrance, he was in the winning Scottish Championship team, and also finalist in the Scottish Cup in Calgary, Canada. There are few major championships in which

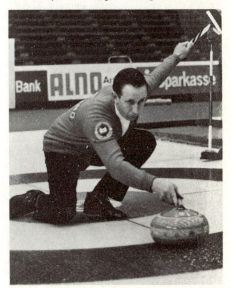

Jim hasn't featured but he has made the British Mixed Open of Hamilton his speciality, winning no less than 7 times since 1968. He has also represented Scotland in the Silver Broom on three occasions; 1972, 1974 and 1979 and was the European Champion in 1979, winning at Varese in Italy.

Ken Watson — *Winnipeg, Manitoba*

Ken Watson is know Canada wide as "Mr Curler" for both his prowess as a player and his enormous contributions to the sport of curling. He is the father of modern curling and the originator of the "slide." With his brother Grant Watson, who ranked as the runner-up third for the first fifty years of the Brier, he was the first man, and is now one of only four, to win the Brier three times — 1938, '42, and '49. He promoted and helped to

organise the first competitive international curling championship (the Scotch Cup) in 1959. Many of the champions over the last four decades are Watson students from his book *Ken Watson on Curling*. Watson was elected to the Curling Hall of Fame in 1973, and his brother Grant, in 1974.

Keith Wendorf — *West Germany*

Keith Wendorf is a Canadian who is the manager of the Canadian Forces Curling Club in Lahr, West Germany. Because he is a resident of West

Germany, he competes for the world curling championship as Germany's representative. He appeared in the 1978, '79, and '81 Silver Brooms and was a semi-finalist in 1982.

Peter Wilson

Peter threw his first curling stone in the rink attached to the North West Castle in Stranraer at the age of 10 and rapidly rose to win the Scottish National Schools Championship in 1976/77. In 1980 his team won the Scottish Junior Championships which led to representing Scotland in the World Junior Championships in Megere, France. Playing against Denis Marchand of Canada in the final, Peter made sure of the Gold Medal by winning 8-5. For the second year in succession the World Junior Curling Championship title went to Stranraer.

Willie Young

In the post-war era Scottish curling was dominated by the Willie Young team of John Pearson, Jimmy Scott and Bobby Young. Willie was Scotland's first ever representative in the Scotch Cup of 1957 and he also became the first Scottish Champion when that competition started in 1959 and won again in 1962. One of the great old men of Scottish curling, Willie is still a regular visitor at the Stirling Ice Rink.

Appendix A: World Curling Champions

Scotch Cup
1959 — (Canada) Ernie Richardson
1960 — (Canada) Ernie Richardson
1961 — (Canada) Hec Gervais
1962 — (Canada) Ernie Richardson
1963 — (Canada) Ernie Richardson
1964 — (Canada) Lyall Dagg
1965 — (U.S.A.) Bud Somerville
1966 — (Canada) Ron Northcott
1967 — (Scotland) Chuck Hay

Air Canada Silver Broom
1968 — (Canada) Ron Northcott
1969 — (Canada) Ron Northcott
1970 — (Canada) Don Duguid
1971 — (Canada) Don Duguid
1972 — (Canada) Orest Meleschuk
1973 — (Sweden) Kjell Oscarius
1974 — (U.S.A.) Bud Somerville
1975 — (Switzerland) Otto Danielli
1976 — (U.S.A.) Bruce Roberts
1977 — (Sweden) Ragnar Kamp
1978 — (U.S.A.) Bobby Nichols
1979 — (Norway) Kristian Soerum
1980 — (Canada) Rick Folk
1981 — (Switzerland) Jurg Tanner
1982 — (Canada) Al Hackner

Appendix B:
Scottish Champions

1959 — Willie Young (Skip), John Pearson,
James Scott and Robert Young.

1960 — Hugh Neilson (Skip), Tom Yuill,
Watson Yuill and Andrew Wilson.

1961 — Willie McIntosh (Skip), Andrew
McLaren, John Miller and Bob Stirrat.

1962 — Willie Young (Skip), John Pearson,
Sandy Anderson and Robert Young.

1963 — Chuck Hay (Skip), John Bryden, Alan
Glen and James Hamilton.

1964 — Alex F. Torrance (Skip), Alex Torrance,
Robert Kirkland and James Waddell.

1965 — Chuck Hay (Skip), John Bryden, Alan
Glen and David Howie.

1966 — Chuck Hay (Skip), John Bryden, Alan
Glen and David Howie.

1967 — Chuck Hay (Skip), John Bryden, Alan
Glen and David Howie.

1968 — Chuck Hay (Skip), John Bryden, Alan
Glen and David Howie.

1969 — Bill Muirhead (Skip), George Haggart,
Derek Scott and Alex Young.

1970 — Bill Muirhead (Skip), George Haggart,
Derek Scott and Murray Melville.

1971 — James Sanderson (Skip), Willie
Sanderson, Iain Baxter and Colin
Baxter.

1972 — Alex f. Torrance (Skip), Alex Torrance,
Robert Kirkland and James Waddell.

1973 — Alex F. Torrance (Skip), Alex Torrance,
Tom McGregor and Willie Kerr.

1974 — James Waddell (Skip), James Steele,
Robert Kirkland and Willie Frame.

1975 — Alex F. Torrance (Skip), alex Torrance,
Willie Kerr and Tom McGregor.

1976 — Bill Muirhead (Skip), Derek Scott, Len
Dudman and Roy Sinclair.

1977 — Ken Horton (Skip), Willie Jamieson,
Keith Douglas and Richard Harding.

1978 — James Sanderson (Skip), Iain Baxter,
Willie Sanderson and Colin Baxter.

1979 — James Waddell (Skip), Willie Frame,
Jim Forrest and George Bryan.

1980 — Barton Henderson (Skip), Greig
Henderson, William Henderson and
Alastair Sinclair.

1981 — Colin Hamilton (Skip), Michael Dick,
David Ramsay and Richard Pretsel.

1982 — Colin Hamilton (Skip), David Ramsay,
Michael Dick and Richard Pretsel.

Appendix C:

World Ladies' Champions —
Started in 1979

1979 Gaby Casonova —Switzerland
1980 Marj Mitchell — Canada
1981 Elizabeth Hogstrom — Sweden
1982 Marianne Jörgensen — Denmark

Appendix D:

SCOTTISH ICE RINKS

Rink	Manager	Tel. Number
Aviemore	A. D. Kaye	0479 810671
Ayr	J. Findlay	0292 263024
Border (Kelso)	G. C. R. Smith	0573 24774
Dundee	D. Reekie	0382 825222/3
Glasgow	Miss N. Wilson	041-423 3093/4
Gogar Park	D. Forbes	031-339 1254
Greenacres	H. McGregor	050-585 633
Inverness	A. D. Campbell	0463 35711
Irvine	S. Robertson	0294 78381
Kinross	G. McCreadie	0577 634678
Kirkcaldy	J. Dryburgh	0592 52151/2
Lanarkshire	B. Wares	0698 282448
Lockerbie	W. Mitchell	05762 2197
Murrayfield	W. Kerr	031-337 6933
Perth	R. Spence	0738 24188
Pitlochry	C. Taylor	0796 3337
Stirling	D. McMillan	0786 64153
Stranraer	H. C. McMillan	0776 2644

Appendix E:
Photo Credits Key

The photographs throughout the text are identified only by an abbreviation. The sources of the photographs are given in full form in the list below.

AB   *The Albertan*
CH   *Calgary Herald*
CP   Canadian Press
CS   *Calgary Sun*
FO   Frank O'Connor
GN   Gordon Nate
IB   Ian Brown
JM   John McKay Photo
MB   Michael Burns Photography Ltd.
MHN *Medicine Hat News*
SH   Steve Herbert
UP   United Press Canada
VS   *Vancouver Sun*

Index